How to Win Friends and Influence People for Teen Girls

Presented by
Donna Dale Carnegie

A FIRESIDE BOOK
Published by Simon & Schuster
New York   London   Toronto   Sydney

FIRESIDE
Rockefeller Center
1230 Avenue of the Americas
New York, NY 10020

Designed by Melissa Isriprashad
Illustrations by Elisa Cohen

For information about special discounts for bulk purchases,
please contact Simon & Schuster Special Sales:
1-800-456-6798 or business@simonandschuster.com

Manufactured in the United States of America

10   9   8   7   6   5   4   3   2   1

Library of Congress Cataloging-in-Publication Data is available.

ISBN 0-7432-7277-3

The names of some individuals in this book have been changed.

To the wonderful young women
who will turn these pages and
influence the future

Contents

PREFACE   ix

CHAPTER 1
Don't Criticize, Condemn, or Complain   1

CHAPTER 2
The Big Secret of Dealing with People   17

CHAPTER 3
Persuasion 101   41

CHAPTER 4
**Everything You Ever Wanted to Know
About Making Friends**   63

CHAPTER 5
Listen Up   87

CHAPTER 6
You Can't Win an Argument   **111**

CHAPTER 7
Admit Your Mistakes   **135**

CHAPTER 8
Putting It All Together:
How to Be a Leader and Get the Best from
Yourself and Others   **155**

Preface

WHEN WE STARTED TALKING ABOUT writing a book just for teens, I said, "Cool. I wish I'd had that when I was a teenager." Of course, there were books for teenage girls back then, but the ones I read didn't seem very helpful; they were full of warnings about misbehavior, rules that didn't make sense to me, and instructions on how to be a "nice girl" (and being a "nice girl" didn't sound like a whole lot of fun). But I did want to be liked, to be more confident, and to be more popular. I wanted guys to notice me and to think I was cool, and girls to include me in their friendships. I wanted to sparkle in groups and to be a leader, not a follower or a loner. But I wasn't sure how to go about it.

Maybe you feel the same way. If so, have I got good news for you! This is the book that will help you learn what it takes to become the person you want to be. And notice I say "learn." That's even *better* news. That means you don't have to be "lucky," "talented," "wealthy," or "beautiful" to be liked. People who are truly successful weren't born that way any more than Tiger Woods was born with a golf club between his teeth. They succeeded because they had an idea of what they wanted and the willingness to work toward it. And you can do the same.

What I hope we can do for you is to give you more information and some tools that you can apply to your life today that can be useful for the rest of your life. The sooner you start (like today!), the quicker you'll get a head start on everyone else. The principles you'll find in this book aren't exactly a secret, but it's astonishing how few people use them, considering how well they work.

This book would not have been possible without the creative efforts of Marguerite Lamb, who collaborated on the research and writing of its first draft. I would also like to thank Paisley Strellis, whose help with the writing and youthful spirit were invaluable in the final stages of this process. They both have put many hours into taking my father's ideas and adapting them for teens. Marguerite and Paisley collected hundreds of pages of interviews with both teens and successful young women, which I think you'll relate to.

And me? I just remember how hard my teen years

were at times, and I'm hoping that by bringing together this team and my father's wisdom, we can offer you an easier and more enjoyable way to learn life skills than my generation had. Write us and let us know how we did! Happy reading.

—*Donna Dale Carnegie*

How to Win Friends and Influence People for Teen Girls

chapter
1

Don't Criticize, Condemn, or Complain

If you want to gather honey,
don't kick over the beehive.
—*Dale Carnegie*

Imagine waking up one morning only to discover that every move you made—from the clothes you picked out to the way you greeted your parents and friends to the questions you answered in class—was recorded on a giant scoreboard for everyone to see. Although you realize that your score is changing how people see you (just like theirs is changing how you see them), you can't quite figure out which choices are increasing your tally and which aren't. In fact, you're beginning to wonder if your place in the world is decided totally at random. It sounds like some kind of nightmare, right? Unfortunately, it's not. Every day, girls find themselves navigating just such a world: school. There are few times in life that we find ourselves more aware of divisions like being in or out, us or them, cool or hopelessly uncool—and so constantly re-minded of where we fall on the continuum.

A recent study looked at students in grades six through ten. Among researchers' findings was that nearly 30 percent of students surveyed had experienced bullying, either as a victim, a perpetrator, or both. As alarmed as I was to hear this statistic, none of the girls we interviewed for this book even appeared surprised—except to say they would have thought the number was higher. Many of them shared their own experiences, including Julie, age 14:

There was a girl in my class named Marie that everyone makes fun of. She's a total perfectionist and always uses the full hour to take a test that the rest of the class finishes in ten minutes. She's obsessed with ballet and all she ever wanted to talk about was her dance classes. Also, it was kind of the way she looked. I tried to be nice to her, but I also par-ticipated in teasing her. She laughed at herself and didn't let people know that she was hurt by what they said about her, but her mom told my mom that she cried every day after school. When my mom confronted me about it, I felt terrible. I told her that I tried sticking up for her, but it was hard. You want people to like you and I didn't want to become a target by sticking up for her. I know how horrible that is. I've been teased before, too. . . .

From Julie's story, we see that she falls into the "both" cate-gory, experiencing teasing both as a participant and a victim. It seems unbelievable that someone who knows how horrible it feels to be singled out and ridiculed could ever take part in doing it to someone else. But if we look closely at Julie's words, we can see that she isn't really putting herself in Marie's shoes, regardless of her past experience. If Julie were truly empathizing with Marie, she wouldn't be able *not* to stick up for her. Rather, Julie is responding to her mom's criticism. Dale Carnegie once said, "Criticism is futile. It puts a person on the defensive and usually makes him strive to justify himself." Or, in this case, herself.

Actually, he felt so strongly about criticism that he always taught the following principle first: Don't criticize, condemn, or complain. It may seem obvious why we shouldn't follow this path when we look at Julie's example. She is indulging in all three big Cs: criticizing Marie, condemning her for her looks and personality, and complaining that she herself can't do anything to help. As tempting as it may be to think that we would never act in such a way, this kind of thinking is, in itself, a form of criticism. We're not here to judge Julie. Dale Carnegie believed the following: "Any fool can criticize, condemn, and complain—it takes character and self-control to be understanding and forgiving." We can, however, learn from her. We all know how rotten it feels to be on the receiving end of an unkind word, but Julie's example also shows us how ugly it can be to know you've hurt someone else. No one wants to see themselves as a cruel bully—or someone too cowardly to go against the crowd. You don't have to make the same mistake yourself; by finding ways to be less critical of others as well as learning how to use negative energy to your advantage, anyone can learn how to deal with tough situations.

✳ GIVING UP JUDGMENT ✳

In high school it's an everyday occurrence to be present when someone is being made fun of or gossiped about and there's probably not a single person who isn't guilty of it themselves.

—Lily, R.I.

IT'S ONE THING TO KNOW we should be empathetic, but it's another to actually *be* empathetic. We're not talking about anything revolutionary here: people have been telling you all your life to "do unto others as you would have done to you," right? So why is it so hard for us to stop and put ourselves in another person's shoes? Maybe it's because the stereotypes we carry around in our heads are a sort of security blanket when we get right down to it. It's a lot easier to make sweeping assumptions about how jocks are dumb, cheerleaders are shallow, and members of the chess club are dorks than to consider each person as an individual—an individual who would no more want to be regarded (or disregarded) as a two-dimensional stereotype than we would. The truth is that the bullying we see everywhere at school and even in the workplace would end tomorrow if everyone from age eight to 108 tried always and honestly to see things from another person's perspective.

This is not to say that you should give up all the opinions, ideas, and perspectives that make you wonderfully, uniquely you. There's a big difference between judgments or stereotypes and constructive criticism that comes from a place of genuine goodwill toward another person. Sound confusing? Look at it this way: even if some truth exists in your complaints about people, snapping at them over their faults—or worse, humiliating them—won't get you very far when it comes to changing their behavior. Dale Carnegie took the example of the world-famous psychologist B. F. Skinner: "He proved through his experiments that an animal rewarded for good behavior will learn much more rapidly and retain what it learns far more effectively than an animal punished for bad behavior. . . . Later studies have shown that the same applies to humans. By criticizing, we do not make lasting changes and often incur resentment." Sound crazy? Before you answer, take this quick quiz to see if you know the difference between constructive and destructive criticism.

Your best friend shows up at school with a nightmare haircut. You:

a) Head to the bathroom with her to see if parting her new 'do differently would make it a little more flattering.

b) Remind her it will grow out . . . eventually.

c) Wait until you're in the crowded cafeteria to tell her she should speed to the mall after school. You hear there's a big hat sale going on.

You love daisies, but your boyfriend shows up with a bouquet of roses on your anniversary. You:

a) Gush over the flowers and tell him they're beautiful—you can remind him how much you like daisies some other time.

b) Thank him and tell him that next to daisies, roses are your favorite.

c) Tell him that if he ever listened to a word you said, he'd know you adore daisies and think roses are totally cliché.

Your tone-deaf sister plans to audition for the high school musical. You:

a) Invite your musically gifted friend over to give her some quick voice coaching.

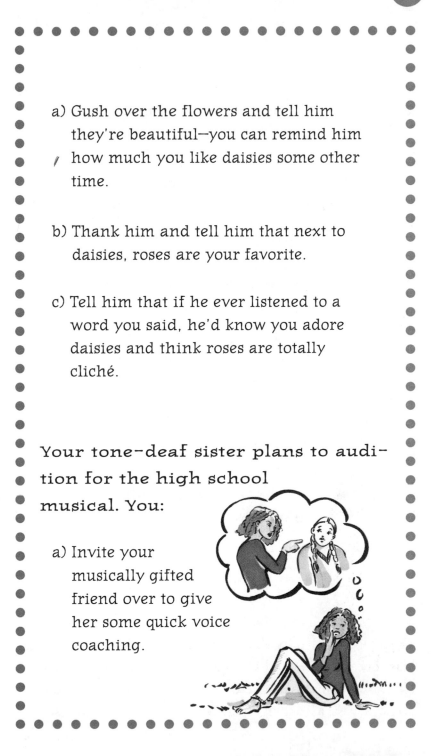

b) Suggest she wait and audition for next semester's (nonmusical) play.

c) Ask her when *Les Misérables* became a comedy.

Your mom overcooks the roast again. You:

a) Eat it anyway. It won't kill you.

b) Push it around on your plate to make it look like you've eaten some and sneak a bowl of cereal later.

c) Ask her if she *wants* you to chip a tooth by continuing to try to eat this.

There are two truths about criticism: everyone's a critic (at least occasionally) and no one likes a critic (even occasionally). Sometimes what we offer as a helpful observation will come across as a judgment. And, if we don't choose our words carefully, what we intend as a constructive criticism can have the impact of a wrecking ball. But unless you've got a chronic case of foot-in-mouth disease, such misfires should be genuine miscommunications and shouldn't happen very often. So, if people routinely flinch before you speak—and you answered "b" or "c" to any of the above—it may be time to muzzle your inner pit bull.

A good rule of thumb is before you say something harsh, consider how you would feel if someone said the same thing to you. Sure, we all get angry. People do and say insensitive things all the time. But look what happens when we dish out negativity.

One time a girl in my high school criticized me on what I was wearing. She said that I looked ugly in it. I reacted by telling her to shut up and go away. I felt horrible, ugly, hurt, and angry all at once. I tried to hold in all my emotions, and all the hurt turned to hate. I hated her.

—Beth, 17, Pa.

Ack! We definitely don't want to end up on either side of this scenario. That's not to say you can never suggest how others might do things better. It's just that when you do so, you should find a way to ensure your words are received in the generous spirit you intended for them. Before you open your mouth, make sure your intentions really are generous. Ask yourself:

———————————

✓ Is the thing I'm about to criticize something that the person can or would want to change? (Hint: This pretty much rules out comments on the way a person looks, talks, walks, laughs, or dresses. Before you cross into that territory, check your motive. Why are you saying this? Your words will likely have zero benefit to either you or your target, will be needlessly hurtful, and may cost you a friend or earn you a lasting enemy.)

✓ Am I about to call attention to something that is possible or easy to correct?

✓ Could my words possibly deter this person from risky or negative behavior?

✓ Do I have this person's best interests at heart?

———————————

If the answer to any of the above is no, then you can be sure the best course of action is to keep your comments to yourself—at least until you can offer them in a more productive way.

＊ USE NEGATIVE ENERGY AS ROCKET FUEL ＊

IT MAY BE HARDEST TO RESIST THE THREE Cs when you're faced with others' negativity. In your life, you will be criticized. People will unfairly condemn you for things you may or may not have thought, said, or done. They'll complain about you and to you. I guarantee it. As you go through life, you'll encounter people who seem bent on dragging you down. You can't control what others say and do, but you can decide how you will respond. You can decide whether you'll let others' hurtful words destroy your mood and torpedo your self-confidence, causing you to take your pain and anger out not just on your critic but on everyone around you. Or you can shake off unfair criticism, put your best foot forward, and prove your critics wrong.

Atoosa Rubenstein, now the editor in chief of *Seventeen*, was only twenty-six when she was appointed to her first editor in chief position at *CosmoGIRL*. At the time, Atoosa faced a certain amount of jealousy, especially from older staff members. To help Atoosa deal with this response, the editor of *Cosmopolitan* suggested she'd gain some favor by reaching out. Rubenstein says: "I sent an e-mail to two people (one of whom is now the editor in chief of another

magazine) saying, 'You have such great experience, I respect you so much. I would love to hear if you have any recommendations for who would be good to work on my team.' Well, one of the women meant to reply to the other, but instead she replied to me and wrote something like, 'Oh, look, the little fashion girl needs a grammarian.'

"Now, the truth is I really see the good in people, so I read it but it took me a minute to see what she meant. Once I did I was really hurt. A minute later she came barreling down the hall and said, 'I sent you an e-mail by accident. You don't have to read it. Just delete it.' She was too late, of course, but I didn't say a word about it then and I haven't said anything about it since—not out of fear, but because I genuinely believe in always putting out a good vibe. I took that negativity she threw in my direction and used it as rocket fuel."

That rocket fuel, says Rubenstein, helped her blast *CosmoGIRL* into orbit and make it one of the most popular teen magazines on the market. The more people criticized her or questioned her abilities, she explained, the more determined she was to prove her critics wrong by making her magazine even better.

You have the same options when you're faced with criticism, condemnation, or complaining—whether it's justified or not. You can counter it with an equally biting remark, which probably won't improve either your relationship with the person or the problem at hand, or you can pause before responding to consider how you can prove the person wrong through a positive action.

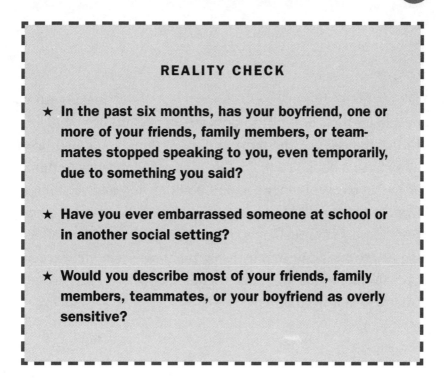

REALITY CHECK

★ In the past six months, has your boyfriend, one or more of your friends, family members, or team-mates stopped speaking to you, even temporarily, due to something you said?

★ Have you ever embarrassed someone at school or in another social setting?

★ Would you describe most of your friends, family members, teammates, or your boyfriend as overly sensitive?

If you answered yes to any or all of the above, you may be pushing people away with the three Cs. On a piece of paper, jot down one or two specific comments you made recently that seemed to alienate, anger, or offend someone. What was your motivation? How did the situation make you feel? How would the situation have changed if you thought about the other person's perspective first?

Next, think of a time in the last six months when someone in your life has unfairly criticized, condemned, or complained about you. What did they say? How did you react? Did you snap back, or use their negative energy for rocket fuel? Write down your answers along with an alternative way you could have handled the situation.

✳ IN THE KNOW ✳

DALE CARNEGIE WAS PASSIONATE about making sure people try their best not to criticize, condemn, or complain. In fact, he claimed the most important thing you could take away from a book like this is "an increased tendency to think always in terms of other people's point of view and see things from their angle." If we are truly empathetic toward other people, we'll stop rushing to judgment about them and offering empty criticism. And by using the three Cs in life, we can become more likable, better friends, and more likely to get what we want from others.

chapter

2

The Big Secret of
Dealing with People

The rare individual who satisfies the heart's hunger
will hold people in the palm of his hand.
—*Dale Carnegie*

If you could have anything you wanted—anything in the world—what would it be? Most of the girls I talked to didn't need long to answer. A nice car, a new wardrobe, and—more to the point—just winning the lottery were all on the list. But as we started discussing their lives with all the crazy, stressful details, the material items they came up with started to fade into the background and something else inevitably came up: they just wanted to be liked and accepted. They wanted to feel that they mattered to other people. They wanted to feel important.

We all want to feel that we're valued. It's one of the most important factors that drive us in life. Without feeling valued, a fledgling Canadian singer might have hung up her microphone when she lost both parents in a car crash, leaving her to raise three younger siblings at age twenty-two. Instead, Eileen Regina Twain kept her family together, continued to perform at a Toronto resort, and was eventually given her big break when a Nashville producer watched her perform. Adopting the name Shania (an Ojibwa Indian name meaning "I'm on my way"), she went on to become, with her third album, *Come on Over,* the biggest-selling female solo artist in history.

You or I may never sell out stadiums like Shania, but we all want recognition, acknowledgment, and attention. It's part of our makeup as human beings and motivates us to do all kinds of things, good and bad. (Think of the bullies discussed in the last chapter—no doubt their cruel behavior came from their need to feel important, no matter how misguided they were.) Dale Carnegie knew that people crave a feeling of importance almost as much as they crave food and sleep. And if you can make others feel they are important, you'll have them in the palm of your hand. After all, if some people are so hungry for a feeling of importance that they'll take crazy risks to get it (more on that

 later), imagine their gratitude if you can make them feel special just for being who they are.

✳ THE POWER OF PRAISE ✳

SO, HOW DO WE GO ABOUT making someone feel like a star? It's easy. Let him or her know he or she is sincerely appreciated by offering up some honest praise. It will boost his or her ego as well as the way he or she thinks of you:

> This girl that I don't really know very well came over to me at school one day and said, "You have the most beautiful hair." A lot of people had told me that she was really nice and I found myself thinking, "Wow, she really is." My opinion of her went way up, and now I always say hi to her when I see her in the halls. I felt pretty good about myself too.
>
> —Kate, 15, Pa.

> I've always looked up to this girl at our school because she is so her own person. Recently I was working an art booth with her and another friend and she said, talking about me, "I love this girl because she is so real. She doesn't put on a show for any-one." Just that somebody saw that, especially someone I re-spect so much, made me feel so good. She's like the nicest, sweetest person ever.
>
> —Stephanie, 16, Pa.

> I'd been having a really bad week—I'd gotten cut in cheerleading tryouts, had a huge fight with my parents, and was feeling generally terrible about ev-erything. I love my boyfriend, but he's not always great at

talking about feelings and stuff like that. So I was totally surprised when he showed up at my house with a homemade card. It said, "I just wanted you to know that you're the most beautiful, smart, funny girl I know. Don't let these things get you down." I didn't think he really knew what a tough time I was having, but he really made me feel special. I still have the card and pull it out and think of him whenever I'm feeling down.

—Tamara, 17, Wash.

Every single person you meet in your life has something to offer. If at first you don't see something, look again. Maybe you've never spoken to the quiet girl whose locker is next to yours, but you love the photograph she has taped to the inside of her locker door. Speak up! There's no quicker way to convince people that you're smart, sensitive, and perceptive than by letting them know you see what makes *them* so special. And not only will you make her day, you'll win, too: it's a simple fact that people like people who like them—and are more willing to accommodate them. Remind people of the treasures they have tucked inside—that might be hidden from others, or even themselves—and you can literally watch someone transform right before your eyes.

A friend of mine used the power of praise to help improve the relationship between her boyfriend and her parents when we were in high school. My friend's boyfriend was less than psyched at the prospect of spending a night hanging with her folks. Okay, that's putting it mildly—he totally dreaded the thought of having to make conversation with them for three hours. He was a little intimidated by her parents, mostly because he wanted so much for them to like him. The result of this nervousness was that he became really quiet and withdrawn whenever he visited her house. Her parents wanted to get to know him, but because he was so uncomfortable, they never saw the funny, smart, considerate guy that she was crazy about. To compound the problem, they were starting to take his stiffness around them personally, wondering if it could mean he didn't like them.

Clearly, the longer this situation went on, the more awkward and uncomfortable it would be for everyone involved. Insisting that her boyfriend "act normal" around her family wouldn't work, so she decided to try something new. The next time he arrived for dinner at their house, she took him aside for a little pep talk. She told him all the reasons she liked him so much—that he was funny, smart, and opinionated—and reminded him that he had nothing to prove. He was truly a great guy. Her parents knew how happy he made her, and that alone was reason for them to like him. Even this brief discussion was enough to get him to

smile and start acting a little more confident and relaxed.

Over the course of the evening, if ever the conversation wore thin, instead of sweating the awkwardness, she would praise someone in the room. She started with her boyfriend, mentioning to her parents how great he was on the football field and that he'd scored the winning touchdown during the last game. In addition to impressing her parents, it gave her father and boyfriend something to talk about for at least twenty minutes. Later, she made a point of telling her mom how good the food was. Her boyfriend jumped right in and asked her mom what was in the sauce. By the night's end, all three definitely felt more comfortable around each other, and after a few more evenings using the same tactic her only challenge was that her boyfriend paid more attention to her parents than he did to her.

✻ THE GREAT THING ABOUT GRATITUDE ✻

YOU DON'T HAVE TO WAIT until your boyfriend, friends, teammates, or siblings do something spectacular to pat them on the back. In fact, the easiest way to make people feel important is to let them know how much you appreciate them for what they already do. Sadly, this is all too easy to forget—especially with the people we are around most of the time. We just expect our parents to parent: to make dinner and do laundry and buy us clothes and drive us to sports or music practice. The same goes for siblings, boyfriends, and friends: we just expect them to be there when we need them. That's their job, right? Maybe so, but should anyone be expected to do their job day in and day out without a word of gratitude? No way! Just think about it in your own life—when you finish vacuuming the living room, don't you want to hear how good it looks? And when you spend an hour comforting your best friend after a breakup, don't *you* feel good when she says, "Thanks, I needed a friend and you've really been there for me"? Of course. Well, the same goes for everyone who is there for you in your life. Just listen to how a little appreciation wowed these two moms:

My sixteen-year-old daughter, Melissa, asked me on a particularly bad day (I'd been feeling sick ever since I woke up) if she could have some friends over to watch a movie. I agreed, against my knee-jerk reaction, to allow it under a few conditions: they'd be out by eleven, no screaming, and please clean up after they leave. . . . I don't want to spend the night in my room recovering. Deal? Well, her friends needed what seemed like a million questions answered, aspirins, tampons, favors, Band-Aids, advice, rides, and snacks. I was compliant but exhausted by 11:15 when the last straggler closed the door. My daughter immediately threw her arms around me and thanked me profusely for going above and beyond our deal. And she told me she'd do one of my chores in exchange the next day. I was shocked—and felt so grateful for her appreciation, I was willing to consider repeating the whole loooong night again some-time. My response amazed me. A little appreciation sure can make for a change of heart.

—Gayle C., Pa.

Hearing this story made *me* think of how many times I've taken my parents for granted. But it's your parents' little, everyday things, like letting you have friends over or having dinner ready when you arrive home, exhausted after practice, that make them *great* parents. Way too often we forget to say thank you, but look at what a difference it makes when we do. In fact, sometimes having great parents is the last thing we want to give thanks for. But remember, when your mom and dad *don't* let you do something (wear the skirt that you know is a little too short, stay out late, hang with people they don't like), they're doing it precisely because it's their job. It would be a lot easier to let you run than fight over every dif-ference of opinion—trust me, they'd rather not spend the evening alternating between yelling and tears. But part of being a good parent is knowing when to say no. Your parents are not keeping you from going to that party just to ruin your social life—they're doing it because they love you and want what's best for you. Even if that may be different from what *you* think is best for you.

Grace and her dad butted heads a lot throughout high school. He felt she made some bad choices, and she got very angry in response. Their relationship got into a bad cycle. Almost anything he said she'd take as criticism and would respond negatively in return. When she went to college, the time and distance apart must have helped. Out of the blue she sent him a card in which she wrote the nicest things, like that she understood now some of the things he'd been trying to teach her. She's still living a very different life than her dad had expected, but that card opened a door between them. She acknowledged that he cared and that his criticism had come from his love of her; she let him know that she thought he had something of value to share. Those simple expressions soothed the troubled waters between them, and—without changing the direction of her own life—helped them to move on to a new kind of relationship.

—Sandra K., Ore.

Okay, you may not want to give your folks a big hug the next time they forbid you from staying out all night, but if you can remember in the back of your mind that they're doing it because they love you, it will be a lot easier to swallow. And who knows? Maybe letting them know you understand where they're coming from and respect them for doing their job as parents will convince them you're more mature than they had thought.

Of course there will be little, less important things you fight over too. Whose turn it is to take out the trash, what happened to the shirt you wanted to wear, or what to listen to on the ride to school. It's inevitable—we will butt heads with our family and closest friends. They're just so . . . available. But these very people—the ones we're most inclined to

take for granted, the ones who see us at our most vulnerable, who see us stressed, distressed, or dressed in our laundry-day finest with a big zit to boot—are the people we need to appreciate most. Our parents, our siblings, our best friends, our boyfriends— these are the people we need to thank most.

We often act as if it's their fate, not their choice, to be there for us. But the truth is, they can choose to be loyal or not, caring or not, loving or not. They have decisions (often tough decisions) to make, and so do we. We can choose to acknowledge their efforts, to offer our heartfelt thanks when they go the extra mile for us. And why be stingy with our gratitude? Giving thanks costs you nothing, while making others feel priceless. Offer sincere appreciation, and you'll feed that "gnawing and unfaltering human hunger," that universal craving every person has to feel important.

✳ BEWARE OF FLATTERY ✳

SO, NOW THAT YOU KNOW HOW EFFECTIVE praise can be, you should head out and start seeing what it can get you, right? Wrong. "We all crave appreciation and recognition and will do almost anything to get it," cautioned Dale Carnegie. "But nobody wants insincerity, nobody wants flattery." Not only can attempting to butter someone up for personal gain be painfully obvious to the person on the receiving end, it's a totally ineffective (and uncool) way of achieving your goals. Just look at these examples.

When I go to the mall, there's always some guy who will start a conversation with me. Eventually he says things like, "You're so hot," and then wants to go do something. And I'll be like, "Excuse me?! How many girls have you said this to before?" It's fake. He's only saying it to me because he wants something.

—Mia, 16, Minn.

Sometimes after people are mean to me or ignore me they'll realize that they've been horrible and will say something like, "Oh, by the way, I really like your shoes." I'm just like, "Whatever . . ."

—Cameran, 13, Calif.

My sister and I both hate vacuuming. Whenever she wants to get out of it, she'll come up to me and say, "Oh you're so much better at doing the rugs than I am. Can't we trade?" I want to laugh in her face, because it's not even a compliment! It's like she's implying I'm more cut out for that kind of work than she is. Like I'm going to fall for that?

—Adrienne, 14, Tex.

The difference between offering a compliment because it's heartfelt and offering it because you want something is the difference between praise and flattery. As Dale Carnegie said, "One is sincere and the other insincere. One comes from the heart out; the other from the teeth out. One is unselfish; the other selfish. One is universally admired; the other universally condemned." Take this quick quiz to see if you can tell the difference between the two:

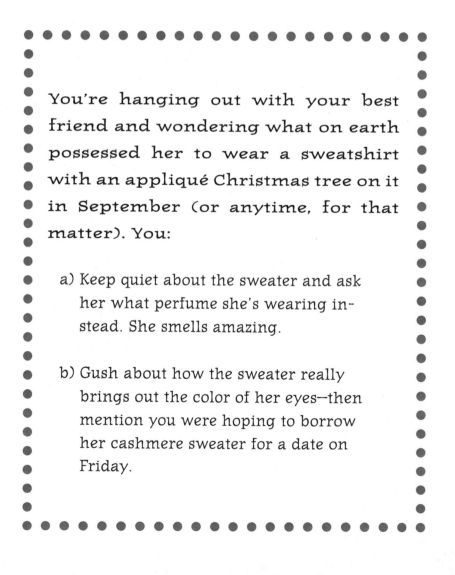

You're hanging out with your best friend and wondering what on earth possessed her to wear a sweatshirt with an appliqué Christmas tree on it in September (or anytime, for that matter). You:

a) Keep quiet about the sweater and ask her what perfume she's wearing instead. She smells amazing.

b) Gush about how the sweater really brings out the color of her eyes—then mention you were hoping to borrow her cashmere sweater for a date on Friday.

On the day of a big exam in biology, the popular girl who sits next to you tells you how much she likes your outfit—even though she barely talks to you most of the time. During the exam, she starts asking you the answers to some of the questions. You:

a) Pretend you can't hear her. The teacher is right there, and you don't want to get caught cheating.

b) Move your paper so that she can get a better look and copy whatever she wants. Obviously she wants to be your friend, and you don't want to mess it up, even though you hate the idea of cheating.

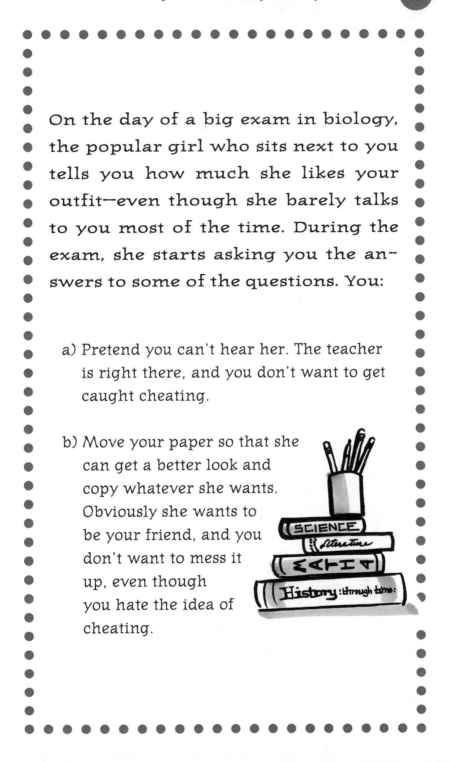

You've been dating a guy you really like for a while, but you're not ready to get physical with him. The last time you went out, he said, "You're so hot. I really like you. I think that making out would bring us much closer in this relationship." You:

a) Laugh and tell him nice try, but he's going to have to value more than just your good looks before you trust him in that way.

b) Make out with him. You know the two of you aren't exactly in love, but it is nice to have a guy in your life and you don't want to lose him.

You're at a party and you see one of your friends across the room. When

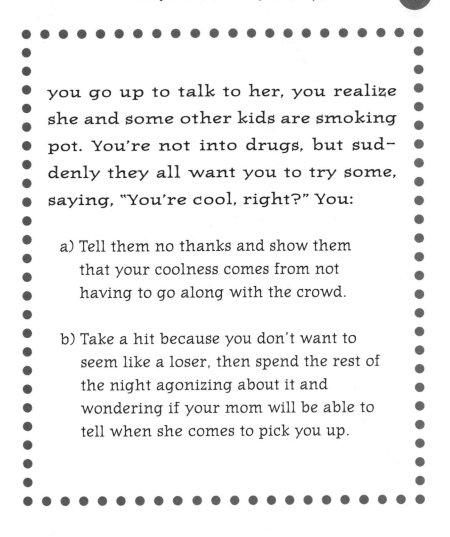

you go up to talk to her, you realize she and some other kids are smoking pot. You're not into drugs, but suddenly they all want you to try some, saying, "You're cool, right?" You:

a) Tell them no thanks and show them that your coolness comes from not having to go along with the crowd.

b) Take a hit because you don't want to seem like a loser, then spend the rest of the night agonizing about it and wondering if your mom will be able to tell when she comes to pick you up.

Okay, it's pretty easy to see that in all these situations people are using praise to try to get something. But we've all been tempted to buy into false flattery to feel better about ourselves. If you answered "b" to any of the above, you need to rethink your relationship with praise. Are you so desperate for recognition and acceptance that you would allow false praise to sway you into doing something you wouldn't otherwise do?

✳ WHAT MAKES YOU FEEL IMPORTANT? ✳

WHILE WE'RE ON THE subject of how best to make others feel important, it's worth considering this: What makes you feel important? What do you hope others will acknowledge, recognize, or appreciate about you? We all want to be recognized for something, whether it's how good we look in lo-rise jeans or how high we score on the SATs.

So strong is this innate need to be noticed that it may lead you to engage in risky behaviors. These include starving or bingeing to be thin, drinking alcohol, doing drugs, or getting too intimate too fast with your boyfriend. Self-destructive acts can be a cry for attention, a desperate plea screaming "Notice me!"

Lots of girls like to have the reputation of being partyers. They drink and do drugs and have sex because it makes them more popular—especially with guys.

—Lily, R.I.

There's a girl at my school who was always known as being a to-tally goodie-goodie. This year she's doing all these crazy things like ditching school. I think she just wants to prove how wild she is.

—Christine, 14, Del.

There is only one way to keep from falling into these sorts of traps: knowing your core beliefs, your nonnegotiable values, and being true to them. If you've never stopped to ask yourself where you get your feelings of importance—the source of your self-esteem and sense of self—take a few minutes to do it now. Write down the things that make you . . . *you*. What traits define you? What are your core beliefs? Your nonnegotiable values?

Now look at what you wrote. Does that jive with the way you're spending your time? Are you living in a way that hon-ors your core beliefs? Your central values? Are you being true to you? If you're feeling overwhelmed by the task, a quick way to gauge how you feel about your choices is to ask yourself how you want to be remembered. Do you want to be thought of as the girl everyone liked? The one who always said hi to people in the hallway with a smile for everyone as she passed? Do you want to be the life of the party—even if it means everyone remembering the times you ended the night with your head in the toilet? Or what about being the popular girl who gained power by making others feel like losers?

Your answers matter. If the way you would like to be re-membered doesn't match the way you think others might recall you in ten years, it's time to work on living more authentically. Unless you commit to being real, no one else will be able to ap-preciate you for who you really are. They can't acknowledge the strengths and achievements that fuel your confidence, that feed your feelings of importance. And if you don't ever articulate these questions for yourself, you can't be sure you're making active choices about how you want to live, instead of just going along with what seems easy or cool.

I'm sure at this point in your life you've experienced pressure to do things you know on a gut level won't make you feel good about yourself in the long run. When you're in the moment—at the party where everyone is getting wasted, or hanging out with a group that torments someone less cool just for kicks—it can be hard to stick to your values. That's why sometimes you're better off using your values to help you decide who you should be hanging out with in the first place—even if it means letting go of a friend.

> There is one girl who I go skiing with a lot in the winter. Last year, at my old school, she was the only other girl who skied. So I went with her, and I guess you could say she's one of the cool people. But she's into doing a lot of stuff that I'm not comfortable with. She started asking me to come with her and do things I knew weren't good for me—like making out randomly with guys and things like that. I just kind of stopped hanging out with her because I didn't want to deal with the pressure of having to say no.
>
> —Ellen, 15, Pa.

Ellen could have gone along with her friend, but instead she listened to her gut feeling, stayed true to herself, and avoided living in a way that conflicted with her core values. It's not easy to do what Ellen did, though. Social pressure is a big deal. We do feel important when we're accepted by those around us—especially someone we see as cool or popular and who might open doors for us socially in the future. And it's an easy out, too, when you tell yourself, "Everyone else was doing tequila shots—all I had was a beer." Or, "I couldn't possibly go to homecoming with that loser who asked me—everyone would think *I* was a dork too." Or, "I was the only girl in the junior class who hadn't made out with someone—it's just what you do." But ultimately you will have to live with your choices. Even if no one else knows what you do, or you never get into trouble, your excuses won't make you feel better when you're acting against your core beliefs.

At the moment we're asked to do something we don't feel great about, we might not believe people will actually like and respect us more for being true to ourselves. But they will. In the end, wouldn't you rather be loved and admired for your kindness, honesty, and great sense of humor than remembered for being the girl who gets trashed and makes out with whatever guy crosses her path? People will notice your best qualities if your way of life lets them shine through every day. And if that means avoiding certain people or situations, so be it. I can't tell you what your core values or defining characteristics should be. Only you can decide that. And, no, you don't have to do it all at once. In fact, we are all works in progress. But remember, the choices you make now help lay the foundation for the woman you will become.

REALITY CHECK

★ What is the best compliment you've ever received? Who gave it to you? Was it believable? Why did it ring true? How did it make you feel about yourself? How did it make you feel about the person who gave it to you? Take a minute to jot down the answers to these questions on a piece of paper.

★ Now try to think of a recent compliment you paid someone else that really hit home. Did the person seem genuinely touched? Did it inspire the person to stand taller or take a chance or simply smile? How did paying the compliment make you feel? If you can't recall complimenting someone recently, look for opportunities over the next few weeks. (Remember, everyone you meet has something to offer that's worth praising.)

★ Make a list of the people you spend the most time with—your mom, your dad, your boyfriend, friends, siblings, and yes, even your teachers. Now make it a point over the next week to thank them for something you usually take for granted, no matter how tiny it is. Afterward note how they react to the unexpected gratitude. How does it make you feel?

★ Copy the list of your core beliefs and values onto a small piece of paper (or create the list if you didn't above). Find a place you can tuck it away so that it will always be close to you, like a small pocket in your backpack or folded into your wallet. If you find yourself questioning your course of action, think about your list. Even if you don't whip it out and read it right there, how does it feel to have your values in black and white, right there with you? Does it help you live in a way that jives with the points you have written down? Does it make it harder to justify going against them?

✳ IN THE KNOW ✳

BY MAKING PEOPLE FEEL IMPORTANT and giving their ego a boost, you can literally transform them. And this doesn't just apply to people you're already close to. Everyone you meet has something to offer. If at first you don't see something worth praising, look again. Reinforce other people's positives and they'll thrive with the attention. Forget about their faults, and these negatives will wither away for neglect. In other words, by acknowledging others' gifts, by recognizing their beauty and their strengths, we can inspire them to achieve their full potential. And by living authentically and being true to your own values, you'll blossom into the person you most want to be.

chapter

3

Persuasion 101

There is only one way in high heaven
to get anybody to do anything. Did you *ever* stop
to think of that? Yes, just one way. And that is
by making the other person want to do it.
—*Dale Carnegie*

Every act you have ever performed since the
day you were born was because you wanted something. Sound cynical? It's not. That's just the way
people work. We're all motivated by self-interest, and there's
nothing wrong with that. Okay, right now you're probably
coming up with a million reasons to prove me wrong. What
about all the hours you've logged doing volunteer work? Or
the time that for no reason at all you did all your sister's laundry? Well, didn't these things make you feel pretty good
about yourself? (And, let's be honest, in the case of volunteer
work—it sure looks nice on a college application.) This isn't
to say you're a bad or self-serving person. You *should* feel

good about yourself when you offer kindness to others. But every action has a motivation. It's part of how people work. You did your sister's laundry more because you wanted the good feeling that comes with acting generously than because you wanted to spend an extra hour folding her T-shirts. Otherwise you wouldn't have done it. It's that simple.

A serious lightbulb should pop up above your head right now, because we're talking about a fundamental tool for dealing with people. In the same way that your wants and needs drive your actions, other people's wants and needs drive their actions—that means your mom, your best friend, your little brother, and even your sweet, wonderful grandma. What we're getting at here is that if you want to persuade someone to do something—anything at all—you'll have to find a way to make them want it too. Sometimes we forget this when we're caught up in our own needs.

After going to all the trouble of getting my license, my parents never let me drive the car. I told them it's totally unfair. All my friends drive anywhere they want! I'm not a little kid anymore, and they need to respect that. It's like they say no for no reason at all.

—Vanessa, 17, Tex.

Whenever I go out with my boyfriend, I feel like we end up doing what he wants to do, which usually means me sitting and watching him skateboard with his friends. I feel like if he really cared about me he'd hang out with my friends once in a while. Or at least check out the movie I want to see instead of always dragging me to some lame action movie that I hate.

—Kara, 15, Calif.

My track coach is totally unrealistic. It's like he thinks that sports are the only thing in my life. When I told him that I was going to have to miss a couple practices to finish a big history project, he freaked and said he'd kick me off the team if I didn't show up. In the end I went, but I didn't do as well as I wanted to on the project. Now I'm thinking about quitting the team anyway, even though I really love running.

—Rebecca, 15, Calif.

Based on what we just learned about human motivation, what's wrong with these three scenarios? None of these girls is considering the needs of the person she's trying to persuade. Stomping your foot and saying you're not a kid anymore does not give your parents any incentive to let you get behind the wheel of their car. Nor does complaining about your boyfriend's choice of activities. (Remember the three Cs from chapter 1?) And while Rebecca's need for study time is legitimate, she's hasn't presented her coach with information to show why it won't get in the way of her performance on the team. Now that we know what's not working, let's look at some ways these girls could adapt their approaches to achieve their goals.

✳ USE A C-BLOCKER ✳

THE NEXT TIME YOU FIND YOURSELF trying to persuade someone to do something, force yourself to stop and ask, "How can I make them want to do it?" Think of this as self-protection, like putting on sunscreen before you head to the pool: it will keep you from getting burned by the three Cs. As we learned in chapter 1, complaining, criticizing, or condemning probably won't get you what you want. Why? Because when people feel attacked, they tend to respond with a surge of pride and defensiveness. That can be enough to keep them from agreeing with you—even if they see your point.

Remember this tip any time you're dealing with an issue on which everyone involved has strong feelings or an emotional investment. Let's take the example of Vanessa and the car. She immediately started complaining about her parents' unfairness. Even if she had valid reasons to drive (maybe it would save her mom from having to drive her to and from field hockey practice), accusing her parents of being "unfair" will put them on the defensive. If, however, she were to start out by saying, "I know you don't feel comfortable with the idea of me driving, but I think I'm ready to take on some more responsibility, like driving myself to practice," she would be opening a dialogue that could address some of their concerns. Maybe her parents' big worry is about her driving at night or with a bunch of friends, but they wouldn't mind her using the car in the afternoon. This will never come out if she starts her request with an attack. Even if her parents don't hand her the keys right then and there, she'll be taking a step toward her goal: convincing them she's mature enough to handle the road.

✳ IF YOU'RE NOT INTO IT, THEY WON'T BE EITHER ✳

IT SEEMS OBVIOUS, RIGHT? But when you're trying to get someone to do something—especially if it's something the two of you have talked about before—it can be hard to focus on why you think an activity is great when your partner doesn't share your excitement. This can be very frustrating, and that frustration can be difficult to hide. Suddenly, instead of extolling the virtues of your amazing idea, you're likely to sound down about the whole situation. Well, guess what, if you're not psyched, it's not likely your pal will get hyped up on her own. But you know what they say about enthusiasm—it's contagious. So use it to your advantage.

Getting excited about something helps especially in situations where the benefits for the other person are not entirely obvious—like Kara's failed attempts to get her boyfriend to do something besides hanging with his boys or going to action movies. Let's get back to motivation: we can say that he goes skateboarding and to action movies because that's what he wants to do. Kara's task is to whip up enthusiasm in him for hanging out with her friends or seeing a movie she wants to see so that her suggestions sound irresistible. Just asking her

boyfriend to sit around the house watching TV with her girl-friends isn't likely to convince him of much. (In fact, it's more likely to leave him with visions of nail polish, gossip, and TRL dancing in his head.) But if she called him up and mentioned that she and her pal Becky wanted to get some friends together on Saturday afternoon for a barbeque by her pool—and that he could bring some of his guy friends too—he'd be a lot less likely to pass it up. Likewise, Kara may never be able to drag him to the latest romance at the cineplex, but if she really wants him to rent a chick flick the next time they're at the video store, she might mention a scene that had her laughing like crazy in the preview. He may get so into the idea, he'll think he was the one to have it in the first place.

* GET ORGANIZED *

THE TRUTH IS, there will be times when all the under-standing and enthusiasm in the world won't help. But if you're a hundred percent clear about what you want and how to make the other person want it too, you can still suc-ceed in persuading that person to your point of view. This happens most often when the persuader is either very per-suasive, intimidating, or both. It's happened to everyone—you start out knowing exactly what you want, but as soon as the other person starts listing reasons against your idea, you get flustered and lose sight of your original goal. The only solution is to be thoroughly prepared for the barrage of rebuttals you think will be thrown your way. How best to prepare? Dorky as it may sound, sit down with a pen and paper and make an outline, starting with what you want, then outlining what you think the other person's likely objections will be, and finally listing your most irrefutable reasons. Having an actual list of advantages to support your idea or approach can be a helpful tool in discussions, giving the other person a concrete reminder of your points. But if it feels too weird to have a list in hand, at least make sure you have all the points fresh in your memory.

The problems Rebecca was having with her track coach are a perfect example of a situation that might have been helped by her preparing a list (either on paper or in her head). She wants more flexibility in her practice schedule but knows her coach will resist strongly when she brings up the idea. On top of that, because her coach is, well, her *coach,* he might be especially hard to confront. Rebecca is used to taking orders from him, not vice versa, so it feels a little awkward from the get-go. But her need for more flexibility is not only valid, it's crucial for her success both as a student and an athlete. She just needs to convince him of that. So Rebecca's list might look something like this:

What she wants: a more flexible workout schedule

Her coach's likely complaints:

1. If she misses practice, she not only won't move forward as a runner, she might lose ground.

2. It's important for her to work out when the rest of the team does so that she maintains a sense of teamwork. She also needs to show her dedication to the sport.

3. If he let people take off practice whenever something else came up, what kind of team would he have?

Why a flexible schedule would actually benefit her coach:

1. Rebecca could offer to do a workout on her own on days she missed practice. She wouldn't lose ground but would save herself the time it takes to get to and from practice and could work out at a time more convenient for her.

2. If she limited her missed practices to once a month, it wouldn't harm team unity. If that statement alone isn't enough to convince him, to show her dedication, Rebecca could offer to set up the hurdles or do some-

thing else for the team the day after she plans to miss practice.

3. By staying up late to work on projects, she's more tired and stressed than she would be if she were able to work out on her own occasionally. That takes away from her athletic performance as much as a missed practice would.

4. Finally, if her other arguments don't get her anywhere, Rebecca could explain that she loves running, but in the future if she has to choose between the sport and her grades, she will choose grades. Then her coach will be out a runner and nobody wins.

Suddenly Rebecca has a very persuasive, very adult argument to present. And by outlining why her plan would be mutually beneficial to her and her coach, her coach would be hard-pressed to turn down her request. It also gives her a chance to think about what she's willing to do to make her position appealing before she's in the high-pressure situation of talking with her coach. Of course, she should never say, for example, that she'd be willing to limit her missed practices to once a month, or set up hurdles, if she doesn't think she can live up to it. The purpose of creating a list is to make sure everyone gains, after all. In the end a list can give you the confidence to enter into any negotiation and achieve the goal of two happy individuals.

✳ WHAT YOU CAN LEARN FROM ADVERTISING ✳

AS LONG AS WE'RE TALKING ABOUT PERSUASION, we might as well take a lesson from the experts—advertisers. The sole purpose of an ad is to arouse in you a want for something. And they work by using many of the same tips we've already talked about, only expanding them to appeal to a whole group of people instead of just one or two people. Just think about your average gym commercial. Is it focused on what the gym wants (such as your membership fee)? No, it points out what *you* want by showing good-looking people with hot abs. And those well-sculpted exercisers are definitively enthusiastic about being there. They're not plodding away miserably on a treadmill, they're bouncing around with giant smiles in aerobics classes.

Finally, by advertising locations open twenty-four hours and super-low membership fees, these commercials counter the most common excuses to join the gym (no time and no money). So, when you find yourself in a situation where you need to persuade a whole group of people, know you can rely on the skills you've already learned. You just need to get a little creative about how you make your case.

Back in my Camp Fire Girl days, I dreaded the annual candy sale. For me, it meant endless door-to-door harassment of my neighbors. I was certain that they were purchasing my mint patties out of kindness to me rather than any real desire for the candy. And I was probably right. Why? I wasn't giving them a reason to want the candy. All that changed one rainy Valentine's Day when I was stuck in an airport. My clever mother, ribbon in hand, suggested we tie a piece to each box and change the sign I was using, which read "Camp Fire  Candy," to say "Need a last-minute Valentine's Day gift? Pick up a box of Camp Fire Candy." It took less than ten minutes for a line of customers to form, waiting to snap up a cutely wrapped box, and within an hour I was sold out. People didn't have much interest in a giant box of candy to eat by themselves in the airport, but they did want a quick gift for a loved one.

Shanetta, of Longview, Texas, used the same strategy on a larger scale to get a business off the ground. It all started when she was just sixteen and her mother asked her to make a mat cover and pillowcase for her nephew to use at day care. It struck Shanetta that her nephew probably wasn't the only kid who needed these items, so she started phoning local day care centers to see if she could show them what she had to offer. "Once I got an appointment to see the directors, I had to persuade them that they needed or wanted what I had to offer," recalls Shanetta. "So I explained how the covers would preserve their equipment and lengthen the life of mats. And if they couldn't afford to purchase the covers themselves, I convinced them that it would be a good idea to make the product available to the parents."

Her strategy worked. At nineteen, Shanetta is the CEO of Nett's Nap Mats. While she specializes in day care bedding, Shanetta recently added to her product base customized fleece blankets, earmuffs, totes, and pom-pom bags for teens. Business has boomed so much in the first three years that Shanetta had to move the company out of her family's three-bedroom house and into a separate production facility and showroom. In 2003, Shanetta earned the first annual Texas Youth Entrepreneur award and was featured in *CosmoGIRL* as one of the top ten richest girls in America. Her success would have come as no surprise to Dale Carnegie: she did everything right. When she approached the day care directors, she focused on what they needed instead of saying, for instance, that she could really use some extra money for college. She made them want what she had to offer—and you can too.

✳ NEGOTIATION VERSUS MANIPULATION ✳

BY NOW YOU MAY BE ASKING YOURSELF if all this isn't just a teensy bit manipulative? In fact, when talking to girls about these techniques, "manipulative" is a word that comes up a lot. But Dale Carnegie didn't mean it that way. He explained it like this: "Looking for the other person's point of view and arousing in him an eager want for something is not to be construed as manipulating that person so that he will do something only for your benefit and his detriment. Each party should gain something from the negotiation." In other words, conducting a negotiation that leaves everyone involved better off than they were before is different from threatening, bullying, or intimidating someone into doing something that serves only your interests. Still confused? Take this quiz:

Your boyfriend has been totally ne-glecting you. To get him interested in spending a little more quality time, you:

a) Tell him you'll rent his favorite movie and order up a meat-laden pizza for the two of you to share Saturday night.

b) Ignore him for two days—no phone calls, no e-mails, nothing. And wait for him to come running when he sees how it feels.

c) Go to a party and immediately start flirting with his best friend. It's sure to ignite his jealousy and have him by your side in no time flat.

Your sister is hanging out and watching TV while you're frantically trying to finish your chores so that you can get started on a paper—that's due tomorrow. You:

a) Explain your predicament and promise that if she covers for you tonight, you'll do her chores tomorrow. And let her borrow your favorite blue tee.

b) Tell her she'll never be able to borrow your tee again if she doesn't get up and help you.

c) Threaten that, if she doesn't do your chores for you, you'll tell Mom about the little accident she had the last time the two of you took out the car.

Your best friend hates parties, but the guy you like is hosting a huge one this weekend. You:

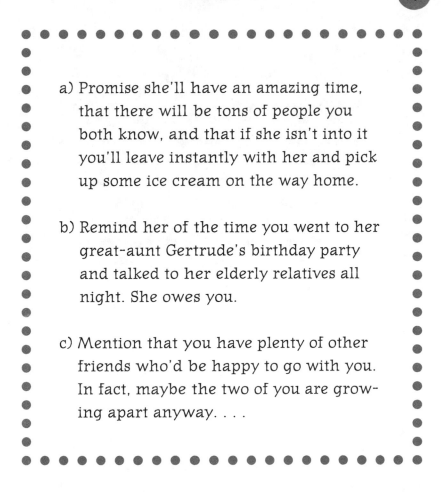

a) Promise she'll have an amazing time, that there will be tons of people you both know, and that if she isn't into it you'll leave instantly with her and pick up some ice cream on the way home.

b) Remind her of the time you went to her great-aunt Gertrude's birthday party and talked to her elderly relatives all night. She owes you.

c) Mention that you have plenty of other friends who'd be happy to go with you. In fact, maybe the two of you are grow- ing apart anyway. . . .

If you answered "b" or "c" to any of these questions, you're forgetting the "mutually beneficial" part of Dale Carnegie's principles. When you both win, it's negotiation, but when you're the only one profiting, it's manipulation. If in doubt, just ask yourself what you are really offering. If "not" is in the answer (as in, "not getting in trouble with Mom"), it's time to rethink your motives. The same goes for offers from other people to you. If you can't see yourself feeling good about your choices later, trust your instincts—someone is trying to manipulate you.

REALITY CHECK

Think about the last time you tried to talk someone into doing something, no matter how small. If the person agreed, was it because you used techniques like the ones we suggest in this chapter, or did you rely on more manipulative means? How did you feel when you succeeded in getting what you wanted? If you didn't succeed, how would you approach the situation differently having read this chapter?

Think about the last time someone talked you into doing something. Did it turn out to be a positive or a negative experience? Did you feel like you negotiated with the person so that you both won, or did you feel in the end like you were manipulated into doing something you didn't want to do? If it was a negative experience, what motivated you?

* IN THE KNOW *

DALE CARNEGIE LOVED TO QUOTE Henry Ford when he talked about persuasion, saying that if there was any one secret of success, it was in the ability to get the other person's viewpoint and see things from that person's way of thinking as well as from your own. Remember, by avoiding the three Cs, presenting with contagious enthusiasm, and being totally clear as to what you want—and how the other person stands to benefit from it—no one will be able to resist your powers of persuasion. Lucky for them, you'll both be better off for it!

chapter

4

Everything You Ever Wanted to Know About Making Friends

You can make more friends in two months
by becoming genuinely interested in people
than you can in two years by trying to get
people interested in you.

—Dale Carnegie

Ι t's hard to imagine anything more terrifying than the first day at a new school. No matter whether it's kindergarten or college, *everyone* feels nervous walking into a hallway packed with unfamiliar faces—not to mention trying to find someone to sit with in the cafeteria. Lucky for you, there's one supereasy way to break the ice anytime with anyone, and you don't have to think of something witty to say: just smile. You'll instantly look more attractive, confident, empathetic, and intelligent. Think of a smile as a power accessory—it says way more about you than anything in your closet. So even if it's the last thing you feel like doing, the first step to making friends is to catch someone's eye and flash them your pearly whites. It's the equivalent of saying, "Hey, what's up? I'm a friendly, confident, approachable person and I'm happy to see you"—only far less awkward than *actually* saying it.

Don't believe me? Think about it. Who would *you* rather talk to, the girl scowling at everyone from under her bangs, the girl who looks at you and then, terrified, looks down at her shoes, or the girl who makes eye contact and has a warm smile? There's no question—you want to talk to the girl who looks like she wants to talk to you. And it works both ways.

My freshman year of high school, I decided to audition for a play. When I showed up at auditions I didn't know anyone in the room and was sitting by myself studying the script, trying not to be nervous. Suddenly this girl sitting like five feet away from me gave me this huge smile. My first reaction was, "Wow, she's really nice," before she even came over and introduced herself. And guess what, we've been friends ever since.

—Kim, 14, Pa.

We've all been in a situation like that—nervously wondering how to find an "in" with a group of people who already seem to know each other. To receive a smile from someone across the room can feel like you've been tossed a lifesaver. So if you're the one who's on the inside, don't forget to extend warmth to someone who looks like they could use a friend. It assures you of winning the karmic lottery—something good will surely come of it.

The truth is, when you're smiling and putting out warm vibes, people not only want to know you, they're more open to your wants and needs too. It's like the opposite of the three Cs. Just take it from Nelia Ponte, the publications manager at Boston University—she hires the yearbook staff each year. Especially because most interviewees don't have much experience (as in, they're students), she gives considerable weight to personal impressions when selecting staff members. "I always notice when the  students smile and are pleasant to the adults. When eighteen-year-old freshmen come in and ask me how I am, I want to hire them right then and there. It shows a certain maturity. To the ones who come in and look around at the walls and mumble, "Hi, I'm here for the interview," I just want to say, "Get a life. Talk to me in a few years when you grow up. In other words, when a student comes in smiling, looks me in the eye, and talks directly to me, it makes me feel like they are confident enough that I'm not going to have to babysit them. Kids arrive without résumés and without job experience, but it doesn't matter. The way they come in and greet me is enough to show me a lot about their character."

A smile and a friendly approach are vital for making friends in junior high, high school, college, and beyond. Whether you've just moved to a different neighborhood, switched schools, or joined a new team, your smile is your admission ticket to new social circles. When you find yourself in any new situation, offer a welcoming smile and you'll be a million times more likely to get a welcoming response. Just think back to what you learned about persuasion: getting people enthusiastic about something makes them want to do it. Well, this principle works when making new friends too. A smile will make you look warm, friendly, and enthusiastic about meeting others—and it's sure to come back to you.

✳ WHAT IS THERE TO SMILE ABOUT? ✳

IT CAN BE TOUGH TO SMILE, and not just when you're freaked about being in a new situation. And let's face it, sometimes your life feels like the lyrics to a bad country song: you're fighting with your boyfriend, your parents want to ground you, you forgot your geometry homework, and it's only Tuesday. Actually, these are the times when smiling can help you most. Studies have shown that a smile is enough to boost your mood, even when it's fake! So if you're feeling lower than the gum on your shoe, pretending to be happy or at least forcing a smile can give you the lift you need to get through the day. Who knows? You may make someone else's day while you're at it.

There's a girl at my school who always smiles. Even if she doesn't know you that well, she'll say hi in the halls and she always has funny stories to tell. You feel special that she took the time to notice you and talk to you even though she has a lot of friends and you might not be one of the people closest to her. She inspires me to do the same—to go out and smile and be friendly to others that I don't know so well, either.

—Lydia, 16, Pa.

Imagine how much less scary the first day of school would be if more people were like that. Crazy as it may sound, smiles have the power to lift spirits, open minds, and even open doors. Not bad for something that takes about zero effort.

There's another reason why your lowest moments are the times you most need to smile. Dale Carnegie explains it like this: "It isn't what you have or who you are or where you are or what you're doing that makes you happy or unhappy. It's what you think of it. Two people may be in the same place, doing the same thing, and yet one may be miserable and the other happy. Why? Because of a different mental attitude." A big part of this "mental attitude" is where you look for your happiness. If you find yourself thinking I'd be happy if . . . I had the right clothes or car or guy or if I could just lose ten pounds or if I could make the varsity cheerleading squad or if I could get into my first-choice college . . . you're setting yourself up for disappointment. Relying on external circumstances for your happiness is a recipe for unhappiness. This is because it never allows you to find true satisfaction. So you get the clothes or the guy or make the team. Now what? Will you be able to sustain that happiness, or will the excitement wear off and leave you in search of something new? Typically, the external thing we think will give us the satisfaction and joy we're looking for isn't so satisfying after all. Just think about all the shopping trips you have been on. Don't those new jeans you swear will change your life eventually become just another boring old pair? Yep. Why else would you continue heading to the mall?

The other problem with using external cues for your happiness is that this approach takes away your control over your own feelings. By contrast, internal sources of happiness do give us something lasting to smile about. You can't help it if you make the team or not—but you are in charge of trying your hardest. Focus on the things within your reach and you'll always have something to smile about. Okay, it's still nice if you make the team, but you won't be devastated if you don't as long as you can take pride in having done your best.

Think about the core values you identified in chapter 2. They should be the source of your happiness, not superficial things like your clothing or the car you drive.

Life as a teen can be hectic and tough, no matter how much you look to your core values for happiness. If you're feeling lonely or depressed and can't shake it, you may need someone to talk to, and that's okay. But you have to let someone know how you're feeling—either your parents or siblings or even a teacher or coach—and they can help get you hooked up with a counselor or therapist. Many schools offer peer counselors and mentoring groups that deal with these sorts of issues. You may also make some friends in the process.

✳ NAMING NAMES ✳

OKAY, SO YOU SMILED at someone and they smiled back at you. Suddenly relief washes over you and you're busy thanking your lucky stars for having someone to talk to (and for the amazing tips in this book, of course), and your new potential friend is saying something but you're too happy to focus on what it is. . . . Snap out of it! In the first two seconds of meeting someone, you'll get a very important piece of information that you must pay attention to: her name. There is no more meaningful detail that we can remember about a person than his or her name, and if you don't capture it at once, it will fade from your memory before you've finished introducing yourself. Seriously, how many times have you been introduced to someone and had a thirty-minute conversation only to walk away and realize that you can't for the life of you remember his or her name? The only thing worse may be discovering you've forgotten someone's name because you called them by the wrong one. Yuck!

We have a freshman class of 150 and I knew twenty coming in. After three months I knew everyone's name, but there are people who don't know mine. It makes me feel like they're not worth my time.

—Sara, 14, Fla.

I've met my best friend's cousin at least six times. The second time we were introduced by someone, I said, "Oh we've met before," but I felt like there wasn't even a flicker of recognition in her eyes. She can never remember my name, even now. My friend swears her cousin is just bad with names, but it still makes me feel like she's blowing me off. Now I really don't like her.

—Tiffany, 13, Ind.

Sound harsh? Maybe, but people really notice when you don't call them by their name. And in truth, if you can remember the names of a zillion actors, musicians, and sports stars, you probably have room in your memory for the names of people you actually interact with. I mean, Theodore Roosevelt had a reputation for remembering the names of every person in the White House, including the maids and the groundskeepers. So did Bill Clinton, and George W. Bush. Now, if the president of the United States has time to learn people's names, what's your excuse?

Most of the time, all we need to do is pay attention, but if learning names doesn't come naturally to you, don't fret. Here are some ways that will help you lock in names like a steel trap.

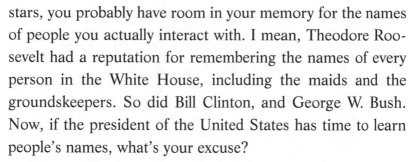

✓ *Listen when you're first hearing someone's name. (Duh.) If you don't hear it well, ask the person to repeat it.*

✓ *Say the person's name back to them, as in, "Nice to meet you, Ben," or "I love your name, I've never met a Zoë before."*

✓ *If the name is unusual or hard to pronounce, ask the person to spell it for you.*

✓ *Visualize the spelling of the name. It can help you store it in your memory.*

✓ Think of something about the person you can connect to their name, like a rhyme ("Alex Dare has nice hair") or a mnemonic ("Eileen has pretty eyes").

✓ If you're really worried about forgetting a name, write it down when you're done talking with the person, along with how and when you met.

✳ CONVERSATION 101 ✳

Whenever I meet someone new, I just freeze up. I never know what to say or how to start a conversation with them. I end up feeling like such a loser.

—Caitlin, 13, Mass.

I'm fine when it comes to talking to my girlfriends, but whenever I'm around guys I get so nervous. It's like, I don't know what's going on in their heads and I don't have a clue what they would want to hear.

—Irene, 13, British Columbia

IF YOU'VE MADE IT AS FAR as getting someone's name, I have good news for you: the hardest part is over. Once you're face to face with someone, talking to them is easy.

Most of us make the mistake of thinking that we have to be interesting in order for others to be interested in us. One of two things will happen next. Either we get so stressed trying to think of something cool to say that we blank out, or we race full speed into a conversation (or worse yet, a monologue) about our latest dieting experiments or our vintage lunchbox collection. Because, hey, if it fascinates us, it must be fascinating to the girl we'd like to befriend or a guy we think is hot, right? Wrong. Dale Carnegie put it bluntly: "People aren't interested in you. They are not interested in me. They are interested in themselves." He didn't mean that we're all self-centered jerks. But we are self-centered—it's part of our built-in survival instinct. Sure, it might be noble if we were all preoccupied by world hunger or human rights or global warming, and we do care about these things, but 90 percent of the time we're thinking about issues that affect our lives directly.

What does this have to do with talking to people? Well, it means you don't have to get stressed about sounding interesting. You just need to sound *interested*. I wish I'd known this sooner. I remember being in high school and dreading being left alone with a guy I liked or a girl who intimidated me (usually because she was more popular than I was). I'd freeze, petrified I'd say something lame or stupid or boring. But I didn't need the perfect conversation starter and neither do you. All you need to do is cast the right lure. So if you're standing in line at lunch next to the guy you have a crush on, toss out a question related to his interests. If he's on the track team, why not ask him what he thinks the best kind of running shoes are. Is he into music? Why not ask if he caught the band that was at the local club last weekend.

This isn't to say you should feign fascination in a complete bore. Nor am I suggesting that you bat your eyelashes and gush over every syllable that escapes the lips of that hunky guy in your English class. It's similar to the difference between praise and flattery: if you're not really interested in what someone is saying, they'll see right through you. But by learning to ask questions and listen attentively you'll inevitably become a better conversationalist—and you may discover the person you're chatting with is more interesting than you'd ever thought. Playing to another person's interests means you'll have to worry about awkward silences far less often when sitting next to someone you don't know that well. Ironically, the most dazzling conversationalists often do less talking, not more.

"So I should just sit there, listening to what others have to say, and that will make me intriguing?" you ask. Well, no, not quite. Listening is not a passive, mindless reflex. It's not like blinking or breathing. It requires your focus. Too often, we miss entire stretches of conversation because we don't pay attention. We get caught up in our own thoughts. Then when a pause does arrive in the conversation, we've missed out on the subjects about which we could be asking follow-up questions. We've also missed a chance to learn something new about someone, and nothing is more impressive than remembering the details of others' interests.

> It doesn't matter if you're in business or in high school, when you meet a lot of people, it's hard to remember their names, their hobbies, and their favorite ice cream flavor. But if it's important to them, you want to remember. It means something, because in this world there are not a lot of people who do that. You really stand out.
>
> —Atoosa Rubenstein,
> editor in chief of *Seventeen*

Remembering what others find fascinating or important can pay off in many ways, big and small. First, we get to feel good about making others feel good. Second, we all like people who like us, it's part of human nature. So, when we admire others, we win their admiration. When we show interest in others, we spark their interest in us. And maybe most important, we set ourselves apart from the crowd in the eyes of a potential new friend.

✳ WHERE DO YOU MEET PEOPLE? ✳

EVEN IF WE ALREADY know a ton of people, we might still feel as if we don't have any true friends. Everyone is looking for someone who they really identify with, someone who really gets what they're all about. Sometimes the trouble is knowing where to look.

I go to a really small school and have known everyone in my grade since kindergarten pretty much. I like people and have friends, but sometimes I just want someone new to hang out with. Someone who isn't just doing the same old thing every weekend.

—Elizabeth, 15, Calif.

It feels like all the guys at my school are only interested in like the same five girls. It drives me crazy. I just really want to meet a boyfriend, but I know it's never going to happen with any of them, and I don't know how else to meet guys except for at school.

—Charlotte, 16, Fla.

One tough part about school is that you don't have much choice in who you spend eight hours a day with. And, especially in the case of small schools, it can feel like you're stuck in the role someone else has given you. Of course you should make an effort to take a genuine interest in the other people at your school—you spend every single day with them. And when you show a genuine interest, you may be surprised to find you don't know your classmates as well as you think you do. Maybe you've assigned them to a category (jock, Goth, nerd) that doesn't fully show who they are.

But you should also keep in mind the great big world outside your school, full of cool people whom you want to know—and who want to know you. Access to that world is

superpainless: just do something you already enjoy. Are
you into drama? Sign up for a
class with a local theater group.
If soccer's your thing, join a
clinic at a nearby college or a
club team with members from
a bunch of area schools. If
nothing makes you
happier than hearing
new bands, find a job
at a record store or volunteer at an
all-ages club. Not only will you get to pursue your interests, you'll definitely run into people who are into the same
thing—and have a built-in topic for starting conversation.
That alone ups your chances of finding someone you really
connect with.

1. Drama Club
2. Girl Scouts
3. Senior Day
4. Trash on Highway
5. Big Sister
6. Animal Shelter

There are literally hundreds of different groups and
places where you can meet people to click with. All it takes is
a little research and imagination. Try looking at your home-
town as a tourist would and start exploring. You're guaranteed to find there's more to your town than you realized.

The Internet can be another great resource for finding
cool things you might not have known about. Maybe there's
an art studio you've driven past a zillion times without even
knowing it existed. Check out a pottery class, and you may
find your inner sculptress, along with some cool artistic people who appreciate you and your work. Or maybe you could
join a Habitat for Humanity group and find some new friends
who share your altruistic nature. The possibilities are endless.

But when browsing the Net, beware. Chat rooms, online
dating sites, and AOL profiles may be a *way* to meet people,

but they're not always a *safe* way. Face it, even if you e-mail back and forth with a new friend, how well can you really know him or her? When you communicate with someone online, it can be really easy for the two of you to pretend to be people you're not. In a way, that's what makes it so appealing: your new pal will never know you're not really the outgoing, bubbly girl you pretend to be online. But that's also what makes it so dangerous. You may feel very close to someone you've spent hours IMing with, but that person may be posing also. So, if you do feel like meeting an online friend in person, ask your parents to meet the person with you. Sound like the last thing you want to do? Well, it is the only way to be safe. Under no circumstances should you meet up with someone you've met online without your parents. It is unfortunate that people may not have your best intentions at heart, but you're old enough to know that not everyone in this world is as good-natured as you are. Be smart, be safe, and be aware. If you don't look out for yourself, who will?

✷ LET PEOPLE GET TO KNOW YOU, TOO ✷

OKAY, YOU DID IT: you smiled your warmest smile, impressed someone with your great conversational skills, and feel like you're on your way to a new friend. Now it's time to take the real leap: open up and let them get to know you, too.

> Every time I meet someone new, I feel like I'm holding back so much. I only let them know like 50 percent of who I am. I don't know, I guess I have a hard time trusting people and don't know how to let down my guard sometimes.
>
> —Danielle, 15, Calif.

Feeling embarrassed, uncomfortable, or nervous about how people perceive us is totally normal. No one wants to feel judged, and if you've ever been let down, put down, or belittled by someone in the past, you might find it extra hard to put yourself out there again in the future. Unfortunately, what we see as protecting ourselves can be a big fat roadblock on the way to making true friends. After all, how can you expect to form a connection with someone if you don't give them the chance to know who you are?

By shutting yourself off from others, you're saying that you're not really comfortable with who you are. So, if you do find yourself throwing up barriers, it may be time to ask what exactly you find so terrible or personal or embarrassing about yourself that you need to hide it away? Chances are the barriers are not as necessary as you think they are. Are you concerned that your love of 50s movies will seem dorky to the guy you like? Or that your utter boredom with shopping will alienate you from your fashion-obsessed new friend? Don't fret. You're becoming friends with these people because they like you. Really. And that means they'll probably like the quirks that make you the cool, interesting, unique person that you are. In fact, they'll probably like you more for (a) being honest and (b) being human. Everyone has something they feel a little weird about sharing with others. It can be scary to break down your walls, especially if you've spent years building them up. But if you give people the chance to like you for who you really are, you can transform acquaintances into deep friendships. And if that doesn't make it worth taking the leap, nothing will.

REALITY CHECK

★ It's time for a little sociology experiment. For the next week, try to smile as often and to as many people as possible. You get bonus points for smiling to people you don't usually acknowledge, like kids you see in the hall but don't normally talk to, teachers, neighbors, the lunch lady. If you're feeling brave, another good target would be the guy you have a huge crush on but have yet to speak to. Keep notes of what happened: Did people smile back at you? Did it spark any conversations? If so, were you able to use the tips in this book to keep chatting? Did you and the other person acknowledge each other the next time you crossed paths? How did you feel at the end of the week?

★ Seek out one activity outside of school in which to take part. It could be a one-day volunteer event like sorting cans for a couple hours at the local food bank, or else sign up for a class or even get a job, as long as you're doing something that really interests you. Then write down your answers to the following questions: How did it feel to be in a new environment? Were you able to use the tips in this chapter to break the ice with new people? Did you meet anyone with friendship potential? How can you follow up with that person?

★ Pick one person you'd like to be closer to. The next time the two of you hang out, try sharing something with him or her that you would normally keep to yourself. It could be something really small, like the fact that you can't stand hip-hop or secretly love American cheese, or it can be something bigger, like an insecurity or a problem you're having. How does your new friend react? Is he or she judgmental or understanding? Did it inspire the person to share something about himself or herself? How did you feel afterward? Was it great to get the matter off your chest? Did you realize your nervousness had been needless?

✳ IN THE KNOW ✳

WE ALL GET NERVOUS in situations where we feel like the new kid. However, smiling (even if it doesn't match our inside feelings) can boost our confidence and will make us more attractive and approachable. Once you are face to face with someone, be sure to lodge that person's name in your memory. Then relax—all you have to do is listen and ask questions to be anyone's favorite chatting partner.

chapter

5

Listen Up

If you want others to like you, if you want to
develop real friendships, keep this principle in mind:
become genuinely interested in other people.

—*Dale Carnegie*

There's a reason a dog is a girl's best friend.
Think about it: your pup is always happy to see you.
He doesn't care if you flunked your chem test or
have a Texas-size zit on your nose—he jumps all over you
and treats you like the best thing since bacon no matter
what. And you love him for it. So what's going on here?
Your dog never sat through a psychology lecture, but he
automatically knows the way to your heart: to make you
feel important and loved no matter what. Now imagine
how well people would respond to you if you showed them
a tenth of that kind of enthusiasm. It's the number one way
to strengthen relationships and to be a better friend, girlfriend, daughter—even a better student. When you show

people your genuine interest in them in subtle ways, the results will speak for themselves. But don't take my word for it. I asked dozens of girls who their favorite person to talk to was, and most of their answers went something like this:

I'd have to say my two friends from elementary school. They really listen and they ask questions.

—Heather, 14, Pa.

I have one really good friend that I became close with in seventh and eighth grade. I can tell her anything.

—Arden, 14, N.J.

My friend Naomi. I can always talk to her when I'm feeling down and just need to vent.

—Rachel, 17, Pa.

Hmm . . . is it just me, or are we seeing a pattern here?

It pays to be interested in whatever is most important to the other person. Friends are really looking for a good listener. This doesn't mean you should withhold comments or that you'll bore a person to tears if you share something about yourself, but the first rule of friendship is learning to be an active, sympathetic listener. And trust me, there's no faking it.

I have a friend who is sometimes good to talk to, but she gets easily distracted. You'll be talking to her and all of a sudden she'll start talking about something else. Or she'll be watching TV and all of a sudden she'll start laughing, and I'll realize she's just not listening to me.

—Jennifer, 14, Pa.

We've all been there. A friend says "uh-huh" when (if she'd been listening to you) she'd *know* the correct answer was "No way!" This kind of half listening is at best annoying and at worst outright offensive. Take this quick quiz to see if you know the difference between hearing someone and actually listening to what they have to say:

Your best friend calls you, and you can tell right away from her voice that she's been crying. At the time, you're IMing with your cousin. You:

a) Tell your friend that you're all ears and sign off with your cousin right away.

b) Sign off with your cousin but start a new game of solitaire—this is going to be a long talk.

c) Write your cousin to explain what's going on. That way she'll understand if your responses are a little delayed.

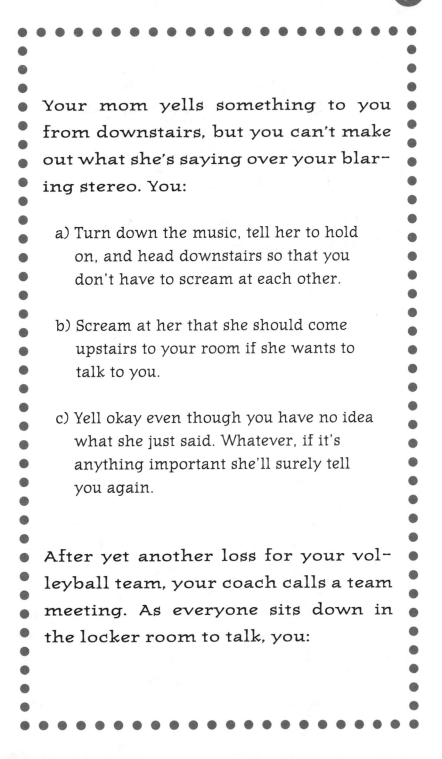

Your mom yells something to you from downstairs, but you can't make out what she's saying over your blaring stereo. You:

a) Turn down the music, tell her to hold on, and head downstairs so that you don't have to scream at each other.

b) Scream at her that she should come upstairs to your room if she wants to talk to you.

c) Yell okay even though you have no idea what she just said. Whatever, if it's anything important she'll surely tell you again.

After yet another loss for your volleyball team, your coach calls a team meeting. As everyone sits down in the locker room to talk, you:

a) Find a seat where you can see your coach and teammates, and look at each person as she speaks. You're sick of losing too, and it's time to find a way to turn things around.

b) Fidget with your shoes while you absorb what everyone says. Hmm . . . maybe a new pair would turn this losing streak around.

c) Sigh loudly and brace yourself for the same lecture you've heard a thousand times. Then sit in the back so that you can discreetly start on tonight's math homework.

We all have moments when we're just too tired, distracted, or disinterested to take the time to listen. And once in a while, it's okay to acknowledge that you're not ready to give someone your full attention and that you want to talk at another time. But if you answered "b" or "c" for any of these questions, your problem is not your mood—it's your listening skills. Listening with genuine interest is as Dale Carnegie says, "one of the highest compliments we can pay anyone."

Active listening doesn't happen automatically (hence, the "active" part), but it is a skill we can master with practice. Here are four ways to start.

Eliminate potential distractions: That means turning off the TV and stereo (or at least turning down the music), signing off from your three IM conversations, and stepping away from the computer. As much as we may think we can discreetly multi-task during a con-versation (especially over the phone), there's nothing more annoying than hearing the telltale mouse clicks of a solitaire game when you're trying to talk with someone.

Get comfortable, but not too comfortable: It's cool if you want to settle into your favorite squishy chair for a conversation, but be aware that your body language will *show* whether you're listening or not. Letting your eyes wander around the room, fidgeting, or yawning can make the person you're talking to feel about as exciting as cold oatmeal. But when you focus in, make eye contact, and lean forward, you make any setting more intimate and show you actually care what's coming out of your friend's mouth.

Ask questions: When your BFF tells you her boyfriend is thinking of going to college two thousand miles away, exclaiming "two thousand miles?!" or "How could he go so far?" will let her know you get the point and feel her pain. By peppering your conversation with questions, you also more easily remember the important parts of what's being said to you ("So it was Janet's friend, Sally, who told him it was a really good school?") so that you can follow up in future talks.

Spot your "I"s: Nothing says "Enough about you, now what about me" like an unsolicited string of "I"s, "me"s, and "my"s—even if you see your comments as relevant. Say, for example, your friend admits that she's actually really jealous of her boyfriend's friendship with Sally, and you respond with "I'm not the jealous type at all." Sure, you're staying on the same subject, but she's not likely to feel very validated—or happy to hear that you don't get jealous. This is a moment when she needs you. Imagine how much better she'd feel if you focused on her and said something like, "Do you really think you need to worry about him? Have you ever told him how you feel?"

Of course we all want and need to share our daily successes, failures, and discoveries. In fact, like we learned in the last chapter, if we're going to develop deep, meaningful relationships with friends, family, boyfriends, or anyone else, it's vital that we do share. But so too is listening. And active listening means knowing when to put others first.

✳ HEAR AND BE HEARD ✳

THE TRUTH IS, listening will make you not only more aware and empathetic—it will actually make you more effective as a communicator. By listening attentively to your boyfriend, your friends, your siblings, and your parents, you'll learn how they think. And you'll learn the best way to make your own points so that they will understand. It's much easier to present a compelling argument if you know what's going on in the other person's head. Recently I was hanging out with a family friend and we were able to solve a problem she was having just by using our listening skills.

Alicia, 15, and her mom were debating (okay, arguing) about a party she really wanted to go to the following weekend. The discussion went something like this:

Alicia: *Look, Mom, this is a big deal to me. A senior invited me to his party—that doesn't happen every day. I don't understand why you're making such a big deal of this.*

Mom: *I know there's going to be drinking there. There's no way I'm letting you get in a car with your friends to go somewhere where there might be drinking. The answer is no.*

After a few more rounds, I took Alicia aside. I pointed out that her mom seemed more concerned about the driving than anything else and that Alicia might be better off addressing that issue than arguing about the "fairness of it all." When she did, she quickly realized that her mother trusted her to avoid alcohol even if it was there. What concerned her mom was the possibility of Alicia getting a ride from someone who had been drinking. Suddenly, Alicia and her mother were faced with a situation that could be solved by compromise. The deal was that Alicia could go to the party with her friends but had to accept a ride home from her mom. And that meant coming home a little before curfew, since her mom didn't want to stay up until midnight just to get her. Was it a perfect solution? Maybe not. Chances are Alicia will be talking to the guy she has a crush on at the exact moment her mom calls to say she's on the way, but at least Alicia won't miss the party entirely and her mom won't have to stress about her daughter's safety. If Alicia hadn't listened carefully to what her mom was saying, she could have missed this opportunity altogether—and probably would have been pouting in her room all Saturday evening.

You never know when listening will help you get your message across in a better way. Listening will help you to be heard throughout your life. Just take it from Nell Merlino, founder of Take Our Daughters to Work Day. It was while she was working on another educational campaign, the YWCA Week Without Violence, that she learned just how much listening counts. Nell told me this story:

> An important goal of the campaign was addressing violence against women and violence among men. We really needed to figure out a way to talk to men—both about how they treat women and how they treat each other. Most of the research we looked at showed that the current outreach programs that were in effect just didn't work. My brother Joe was helping me on this project, and we had a number of conversations where I asked him, "How do men talk about violence when they talk to each other? How do they address this issue?" And he said they really don't. Nobody wants to admit that men hurt women, and most men don't [use violence against women]. We came to the conclusion that part of the reason past outreach efforts had failed was that while most men don't hurt women, most women's organizations were addressing them as if they were all the enemy.

We made a leaflet that was distributed nationwide, not just in a little pile on counters, but by giving it to men in parking lots, subway stations, and other public places. It started out saying, "We know most of you would never beat your wife, your lover, or any woman. We live and work with you. We love and respect you." And it was one of the rare times where I remember—and I've done lots of leaflets for all kinds of things—nobody threw them away. We handed them out at a busy corner in New York City all through rush hour, and even though the sidewalk was littered with other pamphlets that people had tossed aside, not a single one of ours was thrown to the ground, because we addressed men as peaceful people. Instead of tarring them all with the same brush, we were asking them to help us deal with the men they know who come into the bar or the gym and say, "I showed her who was boss," or things like that. We asked them not to let that stuff go by. [The campaign] has been extremely effective and I don't know if we would have reached the same conclusion if we hadn't been working in concert with men.

By really listening to the men she was working with, Nell learned that they needed to be addressed as allies, not enemies, in the battle against violence. Listening rather than lecturing and talking *with* rather than *at* them helped Nell discover a way to appeal effectively to men and succeeded where other antiviolence campaigns had fallen short. She let men know she heard them, and men responded in kind. This is a guaranteed way to make your communication skills—and your relationships—stronger. When we take the time to listen carefully to those around us, we often find our differences to be a lot smaller than we think.

✳ LISTEN AND LEARN ✳

WE'VE ALL BEEN TOLD A MILLION TIMES that if you pay attention, you might learn something. When those words come midway through a lecture on car maintenance from your dad, the last thing you want to do is take them to heart. But unless you already know everything about everything, it's time to stop and pay attention. Here's why: every single person walking this earth knows *something* that you don't. By showing genuine interest in them and listening to what they

have to say, not only will we gain a bit of their knowledge (or at least some insight into how they work), but we also may end up with a new friend.

I'll never forget the first day of my freshman year of college. I walked into the dorm and my roommate had already arrived. She wasn't there, but all her stuff was and I have to say I was less than psyched. Piled in the corner were about a hundred stuffed animals—Snoopy, Garfield, and more Beanie Babies than I'd ever seen outside of a store. Leaning against the wall were some framed posters: Britney Spears, Aaron Carter, and—I kid you not—Kenny G. I wanted to bolt right then. I knew there was no way that my stack of punk albums was going to go over with this girl. I mean, who listens to Kenny G? And when my roommate, Meghan, finally did show up, I wasn't any more convinced that we were going to hit it off. She was totally soft spoken, unlike my usual loud, opinionated friends, and she was wearing a big sweatshirt with a kitten on it. Ugh. What was I getting myself into? I'm pretty sure she took one look at my black nail polish and felt the same way.

Well, guess what? If Meghan and I had seen each other around campus, chances are we wouldn't have taken the time to introduce ourselves, much less get to know one another. But because we were forced to live with each other, we were forced to communicate and get to know each other. And to both of our surprise, we started to become really close. There were some things we had in common after all—like aggravating boyfriends. And even though hers was still in high school (he was a year younger than her) and mine was older, they both lived off campus and we could commiserate at how hard it was to balance spending time with them and feeling like we were still a part of what was going on around the dorms.

We were also different in a lot of ways. She was a water polo player who was studying to be a sports trainer. I was more into liberal arts—English, history, and psychology—and less strong at sciences. When I had to take my bio require-ment, guess who helped me study for tests? Meghan. And when she had a big paper, I was the one she went to for help organizing it. Plus, it was great for both of us to have some-one outside our usual circle to hang with. Whenever I told Meghan about the latest drama with the band I was manag-ing, she always took my side. And when she'd had it with the infighting on the water polo team, she knew that she could look to me for a sympathetic ear. By the end of the year I still wasn't into Kenny G, but I had definitely learned that if I were to judge people on external things like their clothes or taste in music, I could miss out on real friendships. I've lost touch with a lot of people who I was close to my freshman year, but Meghan and I are still great friends—as much for our differences as our similarities.

—Lisa, 20, Calif.

By getting to know each other and setting aside prejudices, Lisa and Meghan were able to fill gaps in their lives that they hadn't even known existed. They learned the value of having an open mind. When we embrace this principle—especially with people who are outside our regular circle of friends— the benefits will always be a pleasant surprise.

✳ DON'T BE AFRAID OF A COMPLIMENT ✳

SOMETIMES WE'RE faced with the opposite situation of Lisa and Meghan—we let the similarities between ourselves and others get in the way of friendship. Remember, when your little sister starts wearing her hair just like you or stealing all your clothes or using your makeup, she's actually paying you the ultimate compliment. She's saying that she thinks you have something to teach her. It's just like the old saying: imitation is the highest form of praise.

I have one friend who has the greatest style. She just puts things together in a way that I never would have thought to—like dresses over jeans or sneakers with a really fancy skirt. Sometimes I'll be at a store and see something that reminds me of what she wears, but I don't get it because

I don't want her to think that I'm copying her style. But sometimes I end up feeling jealous.

—Jane, 14, Tex.

What's crazy here is that chances are the girl Jane admires would be totally flattered if she knew that Jane appreciated her fashion risks. If Jane let her friend know how she felt instead of letting fashion remain a silly wedge in their friendship, she could not only make her friend's day but also have an awesome new shopping partner. Just think back to what we learned in chapter 2 about the power of praise and making people feel important. One of the kindest compliments you can give to a friend is to point out the ways you wish you were more like her. If you have a friend who gets a ton of attention from guys, why not ask her how she's able to be so comfortable around them—and always make them laugh. Does your sister always seem to look more polished than you do—even when she's wearing your clothes? Why not ask her for some advice on how you can sharpen your own look? When you enlist someone's help, you're not copying that person, you're complimenting him or her. In the end you both win.

There are few better ways to win people over than by making it clear that you think they're awesome at something. And that you wish you could be, too. Kassidy, 17, of Des Moines, Iowa, discovered this when she wanted to start her own butterfly business, called Dream Wings. She loved the idea of raising and releasing butterflies but had no idea where to start. She realized her only hope of getting her enterprise off the ground was to do the scariest thing in the world—talk to her would-be competition for a few pointers.

I'd done a lot of research and read a lot of books, but I knew if I was ever going to have a successful business I was going to need some hands-on training. One day I came across a newspaper article about a woman in the area who was raising painted lady butterflies. Someone suggested that I get in touch with her, but I wasn't so sure. I just couldn't imagine someone already in the business wanting to help someone get into the same business, because eventually I'd be competition for her. But after some convincing, I decided it couldn't hurt to try and I gave her a call.

I ended up meeting the most awesome lady, who became my mentor. She wanted me to come over that same evening to meet her and talk. She taught me how to feed the caterpillars, how to take care of the chrysalis, and how to tend to them once they became butterflies. She could not have been more helpful. She even sent me home with some caterpillars and food to raise [them] on my own. She told me I was welcome anytime to help her feed her caterpillars or call her with questions. She let me help her with a wedding release and a church dedication release—she was even my first customer, buying butterflies for one of her releases from me.

Kassidy discovered what Dale Carnegie always taught: we all like people who admire us. By seeking out this woman's advice, Kassidy was inadvertently paying her mentor the highest compliment: showing a sincere interest in what the woman could teach her. When you do this in your own life, not only will you lift the egos of those around you, but you'll improve yourself in the process.

REALITY CHECK

★ Years ago (presumably before the advent of modern privacy laws), a New York telephone company published a list of the fifty most commonly used words in telephone conversations. "I" ranked number one. Surprised? The point is, we barely realize how much we talk about ourselves. It's like biting your nails—you don't notice the habit until someone points it out or you try to stop. Here is a tough exercise but one that will sharpen your listening skills and your self-awareness. For the next twenty-four hours, try to start as few sentences as possible with the word "I." Pay attention to the effect this has on your conversations. Do you find yourself asking more questions? Doing less talking and more listening? Do people seem to respond to you differently?

★ Over the next week, find an excuse to talk to someone you know but don't feel like you have a

lot in common with. It could be the girl you sit nex
to in homeroom or your boyfriend's best friend or
even your older sister. Using the tips you've
learned about being a better listener, see if you can
find one common interest between the two of you.
Start with the obvious (last night's homework, a
mutual admiration for your boyfriends, or, well, the
same parents) and work deeper from there. Were
you able to come up with anything? Did your similarities surprise you? How did it feel the next time
you two spoke?

★ This exercise requires a little bit of courage. Pick
someone you look up to. It could be anyone: the
girl on your cheerleading team who does perfect
back flips; your sister, who can make her al-
lowance last all week; or even your mom, who
manages to balance work, family, and can handle
any crisis—whereas you feel totally overwhelmed
just dealing with school each day. Let the person
know how much you admire her for whatever
traits, and ask for some advice on how you could
be more like her. How did the person respond?
Was she flattered? Did you come away with some
new insight?

* IN THE KNOW *

THE SINGLE MOST IMPORTANT WAY you can be a good friend, girlfriend, or daughter is to listen closely to what the other person has to say. That means getting rid of distractions, listening with your whole body, asking questions, and keeping your "I"s in check. The cool part is that when we do start listening more attentively, we not only learn how to communicate better but can also find friendship and advice where we least expect it.

chapter 6

You Can't Win an Argument

I have listened to, engaged in, and watched the effect
of thousands of arguments. As a result of all this,
I have come to the conclusion that there is only
one way in high heaven to get the best
of an argument—and that is to avoid it.
Avoid it as you would rattlesnakes and earthquakes.
—*Dale Carnegie*

You can't win an argument. Really. And even if you win it, you still lose. Why? Because even if you get someone to wave the white flag of surrender, in most cases you won't have changed your opponent's mind. You'll just have exhausted the person so that he or she says whatever it takes to make you stop talking. Argue and your opponents will come away convinced of two things: you're wrong and you're obnoxious. It's an empty victory because even if you get your way, you will never win the other person's respect. Sure, you may know more than your boyfriend does about music. If you overhear him telling his friends that Bruce Springsteen's *Born in the U.S.A.* is the best-selling album of all time, do you really think you'll win any points by jumping in with "Wrong! Everyone knows it was Michael Jackson's *Thriller*." You may be more up on current events than your best friend, but if she announces that California runs the country because it has the most senators, she's not too likely to thank you for saying, "Duh, every state has two senators." And it doesn't matter if you're the smartest girl in your geometry class—you definitely won't be the most popular if you burst out in giggles every time someone mixes up a hexagon and a rhombus. When you flaunt your brilliance at someone else's expense, you don't gain anything.

So are you just supposed to sit there and smile sweetly even when people are clearly wrong? Well, yes, sometimes you are. It depends on the situation and what will be gained by asserting your opinion—fact or not. If your boyfriend's grandmother is recalling how she survived the Great Depression by selling bits of coal—though she was born in 1938 and the Depression was over by the time she could walk—it's probably best not to call her on it. How will anyone benefit from your history lesson? You may prove your knowledge of U.S. history, but you'll probably embarrass Grandma and make yourself look like a jerk in front of your boyfriend and anyone else in the room. You do the math.

✳ NO ONE LIKES A KNOW-IT-ALL ✳

THERE ARE TIMES WHEN IT IS OKAY—even helpful—to point out a difference of opinion with someone else. When your little brother tells you that *Hamlet* was the best movie Shakespeare ever directed or your friend insists that more people live in Houston than in New York, setting them straight could save them from future embarrassment. You just have to show off your smarts without bruising their ego. And trust me, even if your teacher tells the class that West Quoddy Head, Maine, is the easternmost spot in the United States, you can suggest she may be wrong without looking like a heartless know-it-all. All you have to say is, "You know, you're probably right, but I always thought that Alaska was the easternmost state because it stretches into the eastern hemisphere. Can we Google it?"

One of the greatest thing the Internet has given us—even better than instant messages and streaming radio—is to make arguing over factual matters nearly obsolete. Why engage in a heated debate over whether *Titanic* won the Oscar for best picture or whether Pluto is really the farthest planet from the sun when,  with just a few clicks, you can find the answer? No one—not your boyfriend, your teacher, your parents, or your best friend—wants to hear from you that they're wrong. With use of the Internet, you rarely have to be the bearer of bad news. Plus, there's something far more convincing about seeing a fact on a reliable Web site than hearing it cited in an argument. So be a good sport and look it up, even if you're so sure of yourself it feels like a waste of time. Who knows? You might find out you weren't as right as you thought you were.

I was in the hallway at school, and one of my friends said she wanted to learn Catalan before she went on her trip to Spain that summer. I totally yelled at her in front of everyone, "What are you talking about? They speak Spanish in Spain, you idiot. That's why it's called Spanish." A teacher happened to be walking by and came over to us and said, "Actually, in Valencia they speak Catalan." I felt like a total fool in front of everyone. Especially my teacher.

—Sophia, 16, Calif.

Which is why if you do decide to speak up, you should start by admitting you may be wrong. You have nothing to lose by saying you're not a hundred percent sure but that you have a strong hunch. When you avoid slamming someone for their ignorance, and start by saying something like "You may be right," you will gain four crucial points:

1. You let the person know that you respect his or her intelligence. If you didn't, you'd have no problem dismissing the comment as wrong right off the bat.

2. You admit that you're capable of making mistakes and give the other person the chance to do the same.

3. You give everyone some wiggle room. You'll be avoiding two of the three Cs (criticism and condemnation), so your friend won't feel compelled to defend herself from an attack on her intelligence and will be more open to concede you're right.

4. You'll save yourself from potential humiliation. Face it, if you start out by asserting that you are totally, completely, unquestionably right, won't you feel kind of lame if you find out you're wrong?

In truth, few of us are right as often as we think. And as Dale Carnegie said, "You will never get into trouble by admitting you may be wrong. That will stop the argument and inspire your opponent to be just as fair and open and broad-minded as you are."

✳ FIGHT FAIR ✳

THINGS GET A LITTLE MORE COMPLICATED when you aren't arguing over a concrete right or wrong. I learned this the hard way—and risked losing my best friend in the process—over something unimaginably stupid: musicals.

 Somehow when we first met, the subject came up and she mentioned how much she loved them. I immediately countered by telling her I thought they were the lowest, most ridiculous thing to ever waste someone's time. It then came out that she not only enjoyed watching them, but had studied musical theater for ten years. You'd think that would be enough to make me realize that I was putting my foot in my mouth—but I continued to try and justify my point. And she kept arguing for hers.

After literally *years* of back and forth on this argument (which sometimes left one or both of us in tears), we finally made a pact: no talk about musicals. Why? Because we were feuding over a matter of taste: she loves musicals, I don't. We were both entitled to our opinions, and neither of us was right or wrong. The crazy part is that we often argue about these sorts of things most. And because there is no right answer and no Web page that can absolutely verify either point, these disputes can rage on forever. But you can't win.

The other day my mom and I were at the mall doing some back-to-school shopping. I really wanted this skirt, but she said it didn't flatter my figure. As soon as she said that, I wanted it a million times more. We got into a big fight about it right there in the store. She even tried to talk me into a different skirt, but I was so mad I didn't even want to look at it. We just went home without getting anything and were in bad moods for the rest of the day. When I went back to the store and tried it on again I realized that it didn't look that good, but I would never admit it to her.

—Tina, 16, Calif.

It's amazing how attached we can become to an idea as soon as someone tells us that we shouldn't have it or we're wrong for wanting it. In fact, when someone starts by criticizing us, it doesn't matter if they have airtight logic. All we hear is their criticism. Would the meltdown scene above have happened if Tina's mom had simply said, "I think that skirt is okay, but this one would look cuter on you"? Probably not. But by being unable to back down from the fight, Tina ended up going home emptyhanded and in a foul mood. Not much of a win for either side.

The lesson here: the only thing you get from butting heads is a big, fat headache. And if you really want to get anywhere, you need to learn how to take a step back, cool down, and look for a compromise. Take this quick quiz to see if you're in need of a lesson in the fine art of being chill in the face of adversity.

At the movie store you and your best friend get into an argument about what to rent. This quickly turns into a spot over who's cuter, Tobey Maguire or Jake Gyllenhaal. You:

a) Tell her that you'll rent her pick tonight as long as next week the two of you can watch yours. After all, spending two hours watching Tobey is hardly a wasted evening.

b) Admit the whole thing is stupid and agree to rent a Kirsten Dunst movie instead. You both like her.

c) Grab a stranger nearby and ask her to back you up on the point that Jake wins the hotness contest any day. When she looks at you like you're the crazy one, stomp out convinced that something in that store must turn people into idiots.

Your boyfriend insists that he knows a shortcut to your house, but you're convinced that the two hills you have to walk up actually make it slower in the end. You:

a) Suck it up and go his way. You could use the walk after the pizza dinner the two of you devoured earlier, anyway.

b) Let him know you think it might be a longer route, but agree to go if you can time it and compare it to the other way next time.

c) Walk home the way you want to—even though he decides to take his own route—and pretend you're not home when he gets there. If he really thinks he's so much smarter than you, maybe you're not right for each other anyway.

You're assigned to a group for your French project, but unfortunately the members are more interested in hanging out than getting an A. When you suggest doing a report on the classic films of the '60s, one girl snorts loudly and says, "how lame—they didn't even talk in those. That won't help our French much." You:

a) Take a deep breath and toss out another idea. If you can at least get them interested in a brainstorm, you guys might start getting somewhere.

b) Use the old Google trick to point out that silent films were a thing of the past by the '60s. Then select photos online from the movies you love to show how cool and fashionable they are.

c) Ask the girl how she managed to get this far in life knowing so little, and take off. You'd rather do the whole thing by yourself than be forced to work under these conditions.

Okay, it's pretty obvious that by answering "c" nobody wins, but can any of us say that we've never had that kind of reaction? I don't think so. This is especially true when we deal with "hot potato" subjects like religion, politics, drugs, or other personal choices. It's hard to walk away from an argument, but there are ways to keep a disagreement from turning into a knock-down, drag-out fight.

Welcome the disagreement: Before you say anything, ask yourself if the person you're talking with is pointing out something you didn't know before. Remember what we learned in chapter 5: everyone has something to teach us. You'll definitely diffuse some tension if you can muster up the generosity to say, "You know, I hadn't looked at it that way before." Even if you're not convinced what the person's saying is right.

Question your instincts: Hello! When confronted with the three Cs, it's only natural to want to defend yourself. But if you take the time to question your first reaction to someone's objection, you may find your impulse was to act more out of defensiveness than rightness.

Listen: As much as you may be bursting with counterattacks, always let the person you're talking to have his or her say. Don't interrupt, and let the person know you really hear what they have to say.

Look for common ground: You're horrified by hunting, but for your uncle, happiness itself is eating a buck he took down in the wild. Look for something you do agree on, like a mutual love of the outdoors. It will help you remember that just because you disagree, it doesn't mean you're polar opposites.

Use that ground to stake your claim: Start out by repeating something your opponent has said that you do agree with. Your uncle will appreciate hearing how much you respect hunters' devoted environmentalism even if you follow by saying that you worry the sport hurts biodiversity. It will let him know you're listening to what he has to say and will encourage him to return the favor.

Be honest: If you find yourself being persuaded that the other person is right, admit it! Don't let your pride get in the way of a compromise.

Sleep on it: If you feel as if your discussion is starting to go in circles—or just plain turning into a shouting match—take a break. Agree to think about what the other person has said, then do so. His or her point of view may seem less ridiculous after you've had a chance to consider it without having to defend your own at the same time.

Even if in the end you and your opponent agree to disagree, following these tips guarantees that no damage will be done to your relationship. It ensures that you show respect for the other person's point of view, which can be enough to end a fight on its own.

Recently I was considering becoming a vegetarian. I didn't have a lot of solid reasons, I just wanted to see what it would be like. My mom was totally against this, and we argued for days. I found myself pulling excuses out from everywhere and using reasons to justify myself that weren't even my own, just because I didn't want to admit my mom could be right. She saw right through them. But when I finally told her the real reason—that I didn't have a reason, I just wanted to try it—she was way more understanding and we reached a compromise. She's going to let me try it this summer when I don't have so many demands on my time.

This actually turned out to be a win-win situation in the end, but during our arguments I just felt like my mom wasn't listening to me and kept asserting the same arguments as facts over and over again. ("I'm not cooking a separate dinner, and you don't have time to.") It made me really frustrated and angry, which made me say things I didn't mean. Then she would get angry. I think our compromise was the best solution, and in the end it's something we can both feel good about.

—Jessie, 17, Pa.

Jessie wasn't sure she wanted to go veggie, but she was sure she didn't want her mom telling her she was wrong for just thinking about it. And in Jessie's mom's shoes, we'd probably find that Jessie's initial justifications for giving up meat sounded like a criticism. By stepping back, swallowing her pride, and admitting she may be wrong about the whole thing but that she still wanted to try, Jessie diffused the tension between her mother and herself, and from there the two were able to reach a compromise.

✳ STOP ARGUMENTS BEFORE THEY START ✳

NOTHING WILL STOP AN ARGUMENT in its tracks like agreeing with the other person. You may sometimes even want to do this when you don't agree entirely. Why? Because when you agree on the less important stuff, you keep from getting bogged down by trivial differences and can focus on the things that matter.

My girlfriend and I were trying to decide where our group should go before prom. I suggested an Italian restaurant, and she said that was the worst idea ever. We'd all smell like garlic and she didn't want carbs. It was so stupid. We fought for so long over it, we forgot what the fight was about in the first place. At one point she said she didn't even want to go to the dance with me anymore. Eventually we just let another couple decide. The funny part was, they ended up picking the same place I had suggested in the first place.

—Brian, 17, Ga.

We're all guilty of letting an argument get the better of us from time to time. But imagine how much better Brian and his girlfriend would have fared if they had kept their goal in mind and diffused this argument before it started. She could have said something like, "Italian sounds okay, but I was thinking more along the lines of sushi. It's still fancy, and we won't end up feeling sleepy from eating huge plates of pasta." Hardly fighting words, but they get the point across. By simply avoiding the three Cs, she would have kept Brian from feeling defensive and they could have avoided a battle over the pros and cons of Italian. The fact that she ended up exactly where she didn't want to be just proves the point: you can't win an argument.

Say, for example, your boyfriend wants you to spend Saturday fishing with him. Assuming you don't want to go, you could argue about how fishing is gross, touching worms is vile, and baiting the hook is off-the-charts disgusting. If what you really want to do is go mountain biking with him, why even get into the pros and cons of casting and reeling? You could try this approach: "Fishing sounds cool, but I was actually thinking we could go biking this weekend. They opened a rental shop near the state park, and it might be fun for us to try something new. What do you think?" By beginning in a relaxed, positive way instead of acting indignant, you'll more likely avoid a pointless argument and bring him around to your way of thinking.

Likewise, suppose your best friend wants you to try out for cheerleading, but you think girls should be scoring

goals—not rooting for them. You could tell her so, but what will you really gain by it? Not much, besides letting her know you think something she values is stupid. If you want to avoid both tryouts and insulting your friend, you need to focus on her point of view. Try saying something like this: "I think you'll make an awesome cheerleader and I'm really happy that you want to try out. I'm not sure it's my thing, though. I can't do a cartwheel and I'm not that psyched about wearing short skirts. I'd love to help you with your routines, though, so let me know if you need a constructive audience." This way, you support your friend without imposing your values on her.

Sometimes turning an argument into a winning situation requires agreeing that you were wrong in the first place. If your parents want to ground you for the weekend after you simply borrowed their car (without permission) to make an emergency snacks and soda run, you're not likely to change their minds by pointing out they're overreacting—especially considering you were gone for only twenty minutes. More important, they know you've been looking forward to the dance on Saturday for weeks, which makes grounding you cruel and unusual punishment! Sure, they may trust you behind the wheel when they need a few groceries, but when you need something, they suddenly treat you like a two-year-old. Think telling them so will get you to the dance on Saturday? Think again.

A better strategy: agree with your parents' position and then plead for mercy. "I agree, I should have asked you before taking the car. I understand why you're so upset. But can I please still go to the dance this weekend? Stacy and I have been looking forward to it forever, and she'll kill me if I don't go with her. If you want, you can ground me for the next two weekends, but please let me keep my promise to go with Stacy."

By acknowledging that you were in the wrong, you avoid what could be hours of dead-end arguing over the severity of what you did—something sure to leave your parents more determined than ever to punish you just to get their point across. By admitting right away that you were at fault, you ease tension and smooth the way for discussion, negotiation, and compromise.

If you fail to show someone such respect, your arguing may end up backfiring. The more you mock a person's choices, the more they're apt to defend them. No one wants to hear that they're wrong—not about the clothes they wear, the music they listen to, the friends they hang with, or the people they choose to date. If you think the guy you like might be into another girl, be warned: talking trash about her may get you the exact opposite of what you want. You may find him defending her—and convincing himself of just how cool she is. Bottom line: if you can't be respectful, sometimes you're best off not arguing at all.

✳ LET OTHERS SAVE FACE ✳

NO ONE WANTS TO BE CALLED on their missteps at any time, but it can be especially humiliating in front of an audience. Just think about how embarrassed Sophia felt when she discovered Catalan actually is a language—in front of a whole group of students. When you tell people that they're wrong in front of others, you not only insult them, you also embarrass them and leave them no way to gracefully 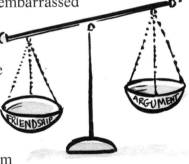 fix their mistakes. What do you gain, for instance, when after you overhear a friend telling someone else she got into her first-choice college, you point out she was only wait-listed? Or if your boyfriend is telling his friends about the sick waves he surfed in Hawaii, will any of them like you more for pointing out his seven-year-old nephew rode the same ones? If your brother invites his new girlfriend out to dinner with your family, do you really need to correct his pronunciation when he orders in French?

The next time you're tempted to correct someone in front of a crowd, check your motives. Will any good come of setting the record straight at that very moment? Or are you really trying to show your own superiority at someone else's expense? What do you really want: to be right or liked? If you decide to correct someone else's mistake—to save the person from future embarrassment—pull the person aside and do it privately. Making a show of it will only make *you* look bad.

✳ ASK THE RIGHT QUESTIONS ✳

ONE OF THE BEST WAYS TO HELP SOMEONE save face is to let them come to the conclusion they're wrong all by themselves. Often when someone tells us something we don't immediately agree with, our first reaction is to make a judgment. We think, "Oh, that's wrong" or weird or bad, rather than trying to see where the other person is coming from. By asking a few simple questions, we can give people the chance to explain themselves—or admit they need to go back to the drawing board.

Say, for example, your best friend wants to get her tongue pierced. You could say, "Yuck, not only is it disgusting, but piercing is so over," but based on what we've learned, mocking her desire isn't likely to get the point across. Instead, why not ask a few leading questions, like, "Do you think it will hurt? What happens if it gets infected? I hear that can be pretty serious. Do you mind if you chip your front teeth? My dentist says that's common." She may realize on her own she has some more thinking to do. The same goes if your boyfriend wants to buy a motorcycle:

"How will you get around in the snow? Do you really want to take the bus for half the year?" Or if your sister tells you she thinks she's ready to have sex with her boyfriend: "Is this something you both want to do? What would happen if you got pregnant? Are you sure he's special enough to be the one?"

If your goal is to get others to think about why they may be headed in the wrong direction, you can be persuasive by letting them figure it out on their own—by way of a few helpful questions.

REALITY CHECK

★ Think back to your last argument. How did it start? Did you accuse someone of being wrong—or vice versa? In retrospect, do you see how the other person might have been partly right? Did you gain anything from saying they were wrong? What, if anything, did you lose? If you had to do it over again, can you think of anything you might have said or done to stop the argument or negotiate a happier ending for everyone involved?

★ The next time you feel your pride well up and you're ready to launch an attack on someone, stop and ask yourself if you're really seeing things from their point of view. Try asking questions to help you—and them—get a better idea of their motives. Did the person come around to your way of thinking? Or were you convinced of theirs?

✳ IN THE KNOW ✳

MOST OF THE TIME OUR ARGUMENTS are more about injured pride than about resolving a problem—and when we let pride get the better of us, nobody wins. But by finding common ground, finding points of agreement, and asking questions to help you and the other person understand the situation better, you can often shut down arguments and open the road for discussion and compromise.

chapter

7

Admit Your Mistakes

Any fool can defend his mistakes—and most fools
do—but it raises one above the herd and gives
one a feeling of nobility and exaltation to
admit one's mistakes.
—*Dale Carnegie*

Sometimes we all blow it. We forget plans or show up for class unprepared or trip and fall in the lunchroom. It's part of being human to mess up royally from time to time—making mistakes is part of the learning process. What matters is how we deal with our mistakes. Even Dale Carnegie—the guy who seems to know everything about how to do things right—was not above mistakes. He lived right near an awesome wooded park, where he loved to take his Boston bulldog for a good run. Sounds totally harmless, right? There was only one problem: dogs in the park were required to be on a leash. He knew it, too—he'd been caught by a policeman before and given a serious warning to keep Rex on a short line. But in his mind the dog wasn't hurting anyone, and he thought the law was silly, so he kept letting Rex run around anyway. Of course, he ran into the same cop again.

But, being Dale Carnegie, he handled it in a super-smart way. He came right out and said he was sorry—*before* the cop had a chance to read him the riot act. He admitted that he knew it was illegal, he had no excuses, and he understood it was the cop's job to fine him. What happened? The policeman took one look at him and the cute dog and said, "Well, maybe if you two stick to the other side of that hill, where I can't see you, we can pretend it never happened." Why? Because in the same way that agreeing with someone can stop an argument in its tracks, admitting to someone that you're wrong can take away their need to prove it to you. (And if you've ever been silly enough to argue with a policeman, you'll know they won't hesitate to prove your guilt with a ticket or worse.) In Dale Carnegie's words, "Chances are a hundred to one that a generous, forgiving attitude will be taken and your mistakes will be minimized."

Just imagine how

much better your mom would take it if you admitted to ruining her favorite sweater before she found it herself. Bring it to her and say something like, "I'm really sorry, I got lipstick on your favorite sweater. I know I should have been more careful, but I promise I'll save up every penny until I can buy you a new one." Chances are she'll understand and let you off the hook. But if one night she has big plans to wear it out, and only learns of its fate after asking you repeatedly to return it, be prepared to face her wrath.

The same is true if you totally forget to call your best friend on her birthday. You may feel so bad that the last thing you want to do is talk to her, but you've got to suck it up. Letting your guilt and her hurt fester will only make things worse. Show up at her door with flowers and say, "I'm sooo sorry that I didn't call yesterday. I'm a total loser and I don't blame you if you're mad at me." She'll probably be ready to forgive and forget. But rattling off a list of excuses—or pretending you don't know anything is wrong—will make her think your friendship is not a top priority.

✳ AVOID THE BLAME GAME ✳

SOMETIMES WE DON'T GET THE CHANCE to admit our faults before someone else calls them to our attention. If this is because you really don't know you've done something wrong, well, there's nothing you can do about it and you'll have to work from there. But if you're trying to get out of trouble without accepting responsibility for what you've done, you'll have to rethink your approach.

It can be scary to take full responsibility for a mistake—especially when someone we really care about has confronted us. It can feel like we're about to lose a friend or at least lose standing in a friend's eyes . . . *forever.* So it's a natural first instinct to reassure the wronged person that we really are the good friend/daughter/sister/girlfriend she knows and loves—only this one time a crazy circumstance drove us to act in a way we wouldn't normally act. But blaming the position of the planets or PMS won't make the other person feel any better about you. Not only will you sound like you're trying to get off the hook, but you will never reassure someone a problem won't happen again if you don't take responsibility in the first place.

Just take the example of Oscar-winning actress Winona Ryder. When she was caught leaving Saks Fifth Avenue in Beverly Hills with $5,500 worth of unpaid-for loot in her purse, she insisted she wasn't actually stealing (or even "shoplifting") but doing research for a role. Did that persuade the judge (or her fans) to say "Okay, well, in that case, don't worry about it"? No way—she got convicted of felony grand theft, later reduced to a misdemeanor (and got slammed for weeks in the tabloids), mostly because she couldn't move past her excuses and apologize. The judge told her, "What concerns me most is the fact that you have been unable, or maybe more appropriately described, you have *refused* to accept personal responsibility for what happened."

Her attempt to dodge blame made the judge wonder: if the actress couldn't admit she'd shoplifted, and that stealing is a serious offense, what guarantee did he have that she wouldn't cruise the aisles again the minute he cut her loose? Which probably explains why mandatory counseling was part of her punishment. You've heard it a million times: she needed to think about what she'd done.

But you don't have to be an actress to know how to put on a good show about why something just isn't your fault. We all feel pushed, pulled, or cornered by outside forces—and use lame excuses like "I wasn't speeding, I was keeping up with traffic" or "I cheated because I just didn't have enough time to study" or (worst of all) "I lied because I knew you'd be mad at me if you knew the truth." All these lines may contain truth, but the bottom line is that you and you alone are responsible for your choices.

I was in the hall the other day and I saw two seniors picking on my friend Belle. They were teasing her for being fat, and she was totally about to start crying. When she came up to me later I told her that I wanted to do something to help her, but I was afraid if I did they would start picking on me next.

—Erica, 13, Colo.

Ouch. These situations are really terrible for everyone involved. But do you think Belle felt any better when she heard Erica didn't stick up for her—or grab a teacher—because she was afraid of ending up like Belle? No.

An excuse will never make someone feel better, so don't waste your time trying to come up with one. If you want to keep people's trust and respect, you need to admit when you're wrong. That's as true for big offenses—shoplifting, skipping school, drinking, or betraying a loved one—as it is for little ones, like flaking on a friend or not doing your chores. As scary as it may seem, saying "I was wrong and I'm sorry" is the first step toward setting things right.

✳ APOLOGIZING 101 ✳

NOW THAT YOU KNOW *WHY* owning up to your mistakes is so important, let's move on to the *how*. Sending an e-mail, IM, or letter is okay if the other person is too upset to listen to you, but nothing beats a direct conversation to show that you really want to make things better. When you're ready to deliver, follow these rules to keep defensiveness from getting the best of you:

1. **Listen carefully:** If you're already in the doghouse, you first need to use your best listening skills. Don't

interrupt or argue with the other person, just let them blow off steam. When they're ready to listen to you, find a time when you can apologize face to face.

2. **Name your offense:** Start out by saying exactly what you did wrong. Did you accidentally mention in front of all your sister's friends that she wet the bed until age ten? Skip the part about how it just came up in conversation. Ignoring what you've done is essentially a nonapology. Start out by saying, "It was totally wrong of me to say that, and I understand why you're mad." For an apology to be successful, you have to let the other person know that you know what you said or did was wrong.

3. **Take responsibility:** If your apology contains the word "if" or "but," you're not holding yourself fully responsible. When you say, "I'm sorry I flaked on hanging out last night, *but* Matt showed up out of the blue . . ." or, worse yet, "I'm sorry *if* you're upset I didn't show up last night, but . . . ," you're not really apologizing. You're accusing the other person of being oversensitive. This pretty much adds insult to injury. If you want to make your friend feel better about the situation and about you, you'll have to start by validating her hurt feelings. That can only be accomplished by owning up to your own guilt.

4. **Express remorse:** "Okay, I flaked, so shoot me!" is *not* an apology. You need to express remorse for your mistakes. Say something like, "I know you were expecting me, and I feel terrible that I didn't even call. I'm really sorry." This is a way to let the person know you get where they're coming from and you want to make things better.

5. **Promise reform:** Your apology is meaningless unless you plan to make an honest effort not to repeat the offense. The other person will want assurances that you can be trusted (which goes back to taking responsibility in the first place). Essentially, you need to include something along the lines of, "I know what I did was wrong and I will try my hardest to never do it again." And you need to mean it. You can't tell your parents that you're sorry for breaking curfew, show them the alarm you've set on your cell phone so that you can't forget the time, and then wander in two hours late the following Saturday. Your credibility will be shot—and so will their willingness to accept future apologies.

6. **Try to make up for it:** Whenever possible, look for ways to undo some of the damage or hurt you've caused. The goal here is not to bribe someone into liking you again but to let him or her know you really care and feel bad about what you've done. If you blow off your friend, why not make plans to do something she loves—that will show you care about her and the friendship. The same goes if your dad is upset that you returned his car with soda cans rolling around on the

floor. Offer to clean it inside and out the next day, and he won't be left thinking you take car privileges for granted. But if it is just some minor offense, like telling your boyfriend his jokes are lame, a verbal apology should do. You shouldn't need to buy him a new jacket or bring him lunch for a week just to make up for your slip.

✳ WHAT TO DO IF YOUR APOLOGY IS REJECTED ✳

UNFORTUNATELY, even the most sincere and eloquent apologies will be rebuffed if the hurt person is still too angry to forgive, much less forget. If the other person rejects your best-effort apology—or doesn't acknowledge it at all—she may just need more cooling-off time. Give him or her a week or two and then try again. Your persistence will show that patching things up is a priority for you. If you're shot down again, you may just have to accept that the other person will not be a part of your life, at least until the hurt heals.

The fact is, we can't control how others receive our apologies—which is why your goal in offering one should never be earning forgiveness. It's awesome if things work out that way, but an apology can be successful even if a relationship isn't fully repaired as a result. Why? Because a real apology is about showing someone that you know you were wrong and that you feel bad about it—not about pacifying someone who is upset.

Too often, saying we're sorry is just a knee-jerk reaction—like after you tell your boyfriend to keep his fleabag dog off you. You say you're sorry not because you really feel sorry for your attitude (that dog is gross!) but because you don't want to spend the weekend arguing with him. You tell him you realize you shouldn't insult his beloved pup (or favorite jacket or new haircut), but you don't entirely get why he's so hurt.

As hard as it can be to admit our mistakes to others, it can be even more difficult to admit them to ourselves. But we all screw up. We all have shortcomings. And we all do and say things that may be insensitive and hurtful to others. Unless we see our mistakes, we can never keep them from happening over and over again.

That's why if you offer a sincere apology, even if it isn't accepted, you'll feel better for having offered it. You know you aren't just blabbing to make someone stop being mad at you—you've actually learned from your mistake. More important, you'll prove to others—not just the person you crossed, but everyone in on the conflict—that you're a stand-up girl who's willing to be held accountable for your actions.

✳ ADMIT YOUR LIMITATIONS ✳

IRONICALLY, it's usually when we try to do everything right that we wind up doing something wrong. That's be-

cause the more balls you try to juggle, the more likely you are to drop one. And if you're anything like the girls I talked to for this book, you're probably reaching the limit of sanity trying to keep everything in your life together as it is. You hope a gazillion extracurriculars will get you into your first-choice college, so you spend hours working out with the soccer team, run for student government, and on free afternoons squeeze in volunteer hours at the local animal shelter. Meanwhile, you make time to do your chores, eat dinner with your family, hang out with your friends, and go out alone with your boyfriend so that he doesn't feel totally neglected. All while trying to keep your GPA up. Hello! With that kind of pressure, there will always be moments when something gives. It's easy to misread an assignment, double book your schedule, or otherwise let people down— but it's not your parents' fault, or your friends'. They aren't expecting too much of you by asking for one spot in your hectic schedule. It's up to you to recognize your limits, make reasonable commitments, and admit when you've dropped the ball.

Take it from Tina, who was just sixteen when she started The Buzz, a Chicago-based research and consulting firm dedicated to tracking what's hot among teens. The Buzz recruits teenage trend spotters and product testers nationwide to keep corporate giants like American Eagle, Nike, and Union Bay up on what teen consumers want. Sounds like a pretty awesome job, right? Well, it is, but balancing a 1.5-million-dollar business while finishing high school at the top of her class and applying to college taught Tina, now twenty-two, a thing or so about admitting her own limitations.

> For most of my life I didn't believe in admitting my mistakes. I always made it someone else's fault. But the older I got, the more mistakes I started to make because of the crazy schedule that I kept. I'd been running my own business since I was sixteen, so I was used to constantly juggling school, sports, and other extracurriculars with what I needed to do for The Buzz, and since I was my class valedictorian, it seemed to me I was pretty good at it.
>
> When I got to college I tried to keep up the same schedule—which turned out to be too much. In addition to classes, I was an editor on the college paper, a member of a zillion clubs, a student-athlete, and trying to stay on top of The Buzz. I even took on running a community service program for the next year's incoming freshmen—that alone would have been a full-time job. My commitments were totally over the

top, and every group I was part of wanted me to make them my first priority. Appointments started to overlap, and I was starting to realize there was no way to do everything that I wanted to.

But I began to resent people instead of seeing the truth: that I had overextended myself. I felt like if they could just be a little more flexible and understanding I could manage. I remember being in a meeting with my community service leaders (who were also my professors) and making excuses for why I'd missed meetings and other functions. My professor told me something that I've never forgotten: "Tina, you've got to admit when you're wrong. The easiest thing to do is say you're wrong and move on. Then it's over. When you start to make excuses, that's when people get angry and it drags on forever. Learn to admit your mistakes."

Since then I've made plenty more mistakes, but I always

admit them. And I've brought that attitude to my business, too. Employees know that I'd rather they admit a mistake than try to defend it. It's helped me be more real and open, instead of a superwoman that can do it all. People really appreciate my honesty, and I have to say, I love that [her honesty] too.

You probably have plenty on your plate too, between school, the demands of friends and family, sports teams, extracurriculars, and perhaps a boyfriend. Don't make the mistake of thinking you can do it all. If you start making promises and fail to come through, people will resent you for the mess you leave behind. But no one will fault you for setting realistic boundaries—in fact, they'll probably respect you for your self-awareness.

✳ LEARNING HOW TO LET GO ✳

WHILE YOU DON'T WANT TO BITE OFF more than you can chew, that doesn't mean you should stick to baby food. A friend of mine once said about skiing, "If you're not falling, you're not trying." It's a fact: the higher you climb, the more chances there are to stumble—or fall flat on your face. But that doesn't mean you should avoid new or scary things because you might not be good at them.

One reason learning to admit your mistakes and apologize sincerely are so important is that they liberate you from endless agonizing over what you've done wrong. So, at your first big high school party you bump into the DJ and knock over one of his turntables. The music stops, everyone in the room stares at you, and you wish more than anything a giant hole in the floor will open up and swallow you alive. Does that mean you spend every Saturday night for the rest of your life alone in your room? No way. You give the DJ your best apology (hopefully before he can tear into you), fix the damage, and move on. Sure, you might get some flack for it, but if you can look people in the eye, own up that you're kind of a klutz, and laugh it off, they won't hold it against you. In fact, they'll probably admire you for admitting that you're human. It will make them feel more comfortable with their own missteps.

But if you hold onto that bad feeling, it can drag you down. Agonize about making a fool of yourself at the party and you'll (a) probably end up so flustered you make another gaffe and (b) only remind people of what you've done. You don't have to live with your mistakes forever, replaying them and punishing yourself over and over. If you admit them to yourself and others, make a sincere apology, and consider how you can avoid them in the future, you're free to try and fail without overwhelming consequences. And in the process, you'll learn to be the person you want to be.

REALITY CHECK

★ Are your apologies sincere? Think back to the last time you told someone you were sorry. What did you apologize for? Did you believe what you were saying? Did you admit specifically what you did wrong? Did you accept blame and avoid "if" and "but"? Write down your experience. How did the other person react to your apology? Did she accept it? If not, do you think that having read this chapter you could communicate your feelings of remorse better? What would you now say or do differently?

★ Start a not-so-dear diary. Whenever you do or say something that makes someone else feel bad, jot down the date and the details. For each journal entry, try to answer the following: What did you say or do? What core value did you violate? Whom did you hurt? Did you know your act or words would be hurtful? Is this something that you think could happen again? Writing down your mistakes—as unpleasant as it may seem—will help you define exactly where you went wrong and give you a chance to honestly evaluate who you are. Do you like the girl who's described on the page? Is that how you want others to think of you? Through this kind of self-analysis, we can turn our mistakes into opportunities for growth. You'll be able to better identify negative patterns and then break them. Recording miscues is also a chance to get them out of your system and move on.

✳ IN THE KNOW ✳

PEOPLE AREN'T BORN COOL or smart or sophisticated—you learn these things through trial and error. The key word here is *learn*. By admitting our mistakes and offering sincere apologies when they're called for, we not only help mend relationships but also learn how to avoid problems in the future. Beating yourself up over mistakes doesn't help anything, either. Remember, mistakes and failure are part of being human. So, if you screw up, do what you can to set things straight and move on. You'll be a better person for the effort.

chapter

8

Putting it All Together: How to Be a Leader and Get the Best from Yourself and Others

No one likes to feel that he or she is being sold something or told to do a thing. We much prefer to feel that we're buying of our own accord or acting on our own ideas. We like to be consulted about our wishes, our wants, our thoughts.

—*Dale Carnegie*

Take a second to ask yourself: Whom do you most admire? Is it a performer known for her knock-out voice and rock-solid values? Is it your best friend, who radiates kindness to everyone she encounters? The president of the United States? Your family doctor? Whoever it is, you can be sure that if the person inspires your admiration, he or she is a leader in one way or another. Something about leaders causes them to stand out from the crowd and bring out the best in other people. As you start living the principles laid out in this book and making them a part of your everyday life, you too will start to show the qualities of a leader. In this final chapter, we're going to reflect on the skills you've learned and how you can use them to get support, bring out the best in others, and be the person you most want to be. Take a deep breath—it may sound like a lot to tackle, but just by getting this far in the book you've proved you're ready for it.

✳ WE ALL NEED HELP ✳

PART OF BEING A REAL LEADER is taking on more responsibility. Maybe you'll decide to step outside your comfort zone and go out for the basketball team (even though you don't consider yourself the most athletic girl around). Or maybe this is the semester you'll get straight As. No matter how you begin to grow, you'll need a support system to help you on your way. And a real leader doesn't demand help, she asks for it. Really. Even the president of the United States can't demand that Congress go along with him. He has to use diplomacy. And you will too. No one wants to be bossed around. We all want to feel in control of our time, our choices, and our lives. (Remember, in chapter 1 we learned that the three Cs are not the best way to influence people.) Just think about it—you'd probably be happy to help your mom repaint the living room, drop off your boyfriend's overdue movies at the video store, or drive your sister to the mall if you were *asked* for help, not *told* to pick up a paintbrush or get in the car. Well, it works both ways. The more we take on, the more we need the help of others to accomplish our goals. And even when our requests seem tiny, it's how we phrase them that will decide if we get the help we need. Unfortunately, sometimes we forget to think beforehand and end up saying things like:

✓ *"Mom, you need to iron this shirt for me so I can wear it tonight."*

✓ *"Kate, you have to help me address these envelopes or I'll never get these invitations out in time."*

✓ *"Jason, you have to fix my bike tire now, or I'm going to be late to work!"*

Here we are, depending on other people to help us out, but we're forgetting the basics we learned in chapter 2—to make them feel important and appreciated. But there's an easy fix for that problem. All you have to do is ask for their help instead of demanding it. It sounds obvious, but especially when we're in crisis mode, common courtesy and consideration can fly right out the window. But imagine the response we'd get just by changing our phrasing in these ways:

✓ *"Mom, if you have time, could you please iron my shirt? I'd really appreciate it; I'm supposed to wear it tonight for chorus and I'm really trying to get all my homework done before I go. You'd really be a lifesaver."*

✓ "Kate, would you mind helping me address these envelopes? I'm concerned that if I don't get them in the
mail today, they won't go out in time for Mom's party.
You'd really be helping me out."

✓ "Jason, could you please help me change my bike tire?
I'm having a lot of trouble with it and I'm freaked out
because I don't want to be late for work. You'd be
doing me a huge favor."

Your needs haven't changed, but your chances of having
them met sure have. People like to be asked even when it's
something they know they have to do. It gives us the sense
that we're in control even when we're not. It also helps show
respect for the people you depend on. As we've learned, feeling important is a huge motivator, and when you ask someone for a favor, you're making them feel important, needed,
admired for what they can offer you, and trustworthy. Isn't
that a lot more inspiring for someone than just to feel obli-
gated?

Another good way to avoid making demands is to take
this tip from chapter 3—get enthused. It's the Mark Twain
approach—when his character Tom Sawyer wanted to get
out of painting a fence, did he complain to all his friends
about what a drag it was? No, he pretended it was the coolest
thing this side of iPods (okay, so that's an anachronism, but
work with me here). Pretty soon, he had a ton of guys fight-

ing to do his work for him. By getting his friends excited about the job, he didn't even have to ask for their help, much less demand it.

Holly, a tenth-grader from Pennsylvania, learned the importance of inspiring enthusiasm after taking a Dale Carnegie "Generation Next" course aimed at helping teens build confidence and leadership skills. In charge of her school's Publications Room, Holly needed to light a fire under her staff:

In the pub room I once again sat trying to get my staff to work. No one wanted to do any of the stuff that needed doing, and I wasn't having any luck motivating them. Then I remembered Dale Carnegie and his stories about enthusiasm. I decided to try it with my staff to see if the enthusiasm would spread from me to them. I became really animated and positive about the work I was giving them, no matter how petty it may have seemed. I treated each job like it was the most important in the world. As [the staff] began to bring their work back to me completed, I noticed a definite change in some of their attitudes. When they finished with something, I made sure to tell the person what a great job they'd done and thank them for their help. This made most of the staff even more enthusiastic about and eager to do the work I assigned to them later. This

was a huge breakthrough, and I feel like I've gained the enthusiasm and the cooperation of most of the staff.

Sure, the work needed to get done, but Holly showed her
leadership skills by using enthusiasm instead of criticism,
threats, badgering, or bullying to get her staff behind her. She
made each member feel important and she trusted them all to
get the job done.

✳ DON'T MICROMANAGE ✳

IT'S POINTLESS TO ASK FOR SOMETHING persuasively
only to start dictating orders once you get someone to agree.
The best leaders know how to make asking for help sound
like the compliment it is. Remember, you want people to feel
important, needed, admired, *and* trustworthy. How enthusiastic would Holly's staff have been if, after doling out the
tasks, she checked up on them every two seconds? Not very.
But by trusting them, she made them feel important and
helpful—not like indentured servants.

This idea counts twice as much when you're asking for
smaller favors. If you ask your sister to please throw your
laundry in with hers, don't add, "Make sure you use the
scent-free detergent, cold water, and two dryer sheets." And
if you really want her help addressing the envelopes, don't
freak out if she puts the return address on the front instead of
the back. Do you want your friend to talk to your boyfriend
and see why he's been acting so weird lately? Then don't give

her a script. If you trust her enough to be the go-between, you can trust her to say the right things.

It's important to give people the freedom to respond to your requests in their own ways. And, who knows, they may just surprise you with their creativity.

I like to be in charge a lot. Recently I did a project with someone in my biology class, and she turned out to be equally into taking charge. She told me everything we needed to do—she had it all planned out. I was just really upset that she wanted me to do all this work but couldn't be bothered to really listen to any of my input. She would ask me questions and I would make suggestions, but then she would show me how her ideas were better and ignore everything I said. It really annoyed me.

—Kate, 15, Pa.

Well, yeah, that would annoy anybody. People want to feel like you're asking for their help and input because you respect their intelligence, creativity, abilities, or judgment. By failing to do this, Kate's partner was not only being insulting, she also missed out on Kate's potentially great ideas that her partner may never have thought of. Maybe Kate had a super-creative way to display their results or a technique that would cut their experimenting time in half. Her partner will never know, because she didn't give Kate the common courtesy of really listening to her. When we micromanage, we forget a number one rule of active listening: to remember that everyone has something to offer and some new light to shed on a situation. Sure, they may want to do things differently from how we do them, but that's how creativity and progress happen. The next time you enlist someone's help, show respect for their talents by letting them do their own thing. Chances are you'll both come out on top.

✳ GIVE CREDIT WHERE IT'S DUE— AND SOMETIMES WHERE IT'S NOT ✳

OKAY, SO YOU'VE USED YOUR BEST persuasive skills to get people behind you, and you finally got the help you were looking for. You still have one important step: graciously giving the person credit and letting them (and others) know you really appreciate what they've done for you. Does your dad tell you how nice you look on your way out the door to your chorus performance? Let him know you owe it to your mom for ironing your shirt. And if your mom gives you a big hug to thank you for organizing her birthday party, don't forget to let her know you'd never have gotten the invitations out on time without your sister's help. Do you make it to work just in the nick of time? When your boss comments that you're out of breath, what does it cost to say, "Yeah, I almost didn't make it, but my brother helped me fix my bike so I wouldn't be late"? Nothing at all. It doesn't matter if the person you're acknowledging is around to hear the praise or not. (You gave them a big thank-you at the time, right?) By letting others know of the role someone has played in your success, you all win. Positive comments have a way of getting back to people just as much as negative ones do. When your mom, sister, or brother hear secondhand that you valued their efforts, the compliment means even more than if they hear it from you. And even if they don't, you're raising others' opinions of them through your words—and of yourself by showing that you're humble enough to give credit where it's due.

As CEO of Girl Scouts of America, Frances Hesselbein knows a thing or two about being a leader. But when she sat down with our writers to discuss some of the changes she made to bring the organization into the twenty-first century, she didn't want to talk about herself. She focused instead on the accomplishments of others: "One person never transforms anything. It's always the people of the organization working together who transform or make remarkable changes in an organization." Under her leadership, the Girl Scouts tripled minority membership. "People try to give me credit for that, but you do not sit at a desk in New York and say, 'Let there be diversity.' It happens because you have 700,000 remarkable volunteers around the country who mobilize around the mission, who are inspired by a specific goal, and *they* do it." Obviously "they" have to be guided by an effective leader—one who knows how to ask for things and get them done. But by giving credit to her employees and volunteers, Frances Hesselbein shows why she's exactly that kind of leader: she knows that making others feel important for their contribution far outweighs the benefits of basking alone in praise.

If you're truly skilled at giving credit, you may just be able to convince others that something *you* want was their idea in the first place. Do you want to start an Amnesty International Club at your school, but your friends think that volunteer work is a drag? Why not tell them some stories about people AI has helped. After they hear about a single mother being rescued in the Middle East, they may come to the conclusion "on their own" that they need to be involved with the club

right away. Does it really matter who takes the credit if your main goal, founding a volunteer group, is accomplished? No, not one bit—especially if you suddenly have a bunch of energized, enthusiastic workers at your side.

Of course, this tactic works for smaller things too. Say you found the perfect prom dress—but it costs $100 more than your mom is willing to spend. You could demand that she buy it for you, insisting your life will be ruined if she doesn't, but how far will that really get you? Consider plan B: go with Mom to the store, model the dream dress for her, and say, "I love it, but I know it's more than you said I could spend. I just can't find another one like it. If I'd already started my summer job, I could pay for the difference. I'm so bummed, I'll have the money in like two weeks. I wonder if the lifeguard manager would give me an advance. . . ." Unless you're already in debt to her, chances are your mom will save the day with a loan. Best of all, instead of trying to argue her into backing down on her original price limit, you give her the chance to be the hero. Everybody wins.

Likewise, suppose your boyfriend has a standing date each month with his guy friends to go to a baseball game. You could stomp your foot and insist that if he really loved you he'd take you with them, but he may resent your infringing

on his guy time. Instead, the next time you two are watching a game on TV, you could say, "You know, I have a really hard time getting into the sport this way. It seems like it'd be a lot more fun to actually be there with the crowd cheering and all the action right in front of you. In fact, I can't believe that I've lived so close to Boston my whole life and have never been inside Fenway Park. It's like a major landmark, right? What's it like when you go?" Unless he's hopelessly obtuse—or really, really doesn't want to give up his guy time—he should get the hint. And he'll probably be way more psyched to have you tag along if he makes the suggestion, rather than feeling you forced him into it.

If you remember your goal, who takes credit means a lot less than getting it accomplished in the end. By asking questions and making suggestions, you'll guide the other person to a certain conclusion rather than dragging him or her kicking and screaming. Others are always more likely to come around to your way of thinking if they get there on their own two feet.

✳ BRING OUT THE BEST IN PEOPLE: RAISE THE BAR ✳

FOR BETTER OR WORSE, we all tend to believe our own press. That is, we generally believe we're as good or as bad as others say we are. Just think about it. If you think (or suspect) that your parents consider you their "artistic" daughter while your sister is the smart one, and you know they won't raise an eyebrow when you bring home a less than stellar report card, are you going to make an extra effort to get an A next time? Maybe, but you also may feel their expectations don't make it worth your time and hard work.

On the other hand, how do you feel when your boyfriend tells you he thinks you're the funniest girl alive, or your best friend raves about how dependable

you are, or you overhear your mom telling your dad that she knows you always tell her the truth? Doesn't it inspire you to be your most hilarious, upbeat self around your guy, or bend over backward to help your friend, or feel duty-bound to tell your mom the whole truth and nothing but?

If you're like 99 percent of the people on the planet, the answer is yes. People have a way of rising or falling to meet what is expected of them. Set the bar high and they'll strive to jump over it; set it low and they'll sink as deep as they can get away with. Expecting the best of people works the same way that praising them does (remember chapter 2?): it inspires them to live up to their full potential.

Are you worried about your boyfriend getting interested in another girl while you're away for four weeks this summer? You could be clingy and paranoid in the days before you leave, but that's not a very attractive portrait for him to remember you by. Besides, he may feel truly hurt at your lack of faith in him. If instead you let him know how much you care about him, just what a great boyfriend he is, and how lucky you feel to have found someone you can really trust, you'll inspire him to live up to your expectations and be a better man.

Do you think one of your friends might have gossiped about you behind your back? (How else would the whole school seem to know about your recent trips to a shrink?) You could confront her, but even if the rumor's true she's likely to deny it. And if you are off base, imagine how hurt she'd be. Why not let her know that you value her friendship and say something like, "It's so important to me to have someone I can talk to without worrying that you'll ever tell anyone. It hurts so much when people gossip, and it means a lot to me that you'd never do that." If she really is your friend, she'll respect your privacy more than ever—whether or not she spilled the beans in the first place.

✳ THE POWER OF FAITH ✳

EXPECTING THE BEST IS A GREAT WAY to get others to come through for you, but it isn't just about you. Sometimes the real payoff is seeing people you care about succeed in something that's important to them. Tell someone you think she's smart enough, strong enough, fast enough to accomplish what they have in front of them, and they'll be halfway there.

Every day before my midterms last January, my boyfriend would send me a cute e-mail telling me he knew I could handle it like the pro that I am. It's a really nice boost of confidence.

Even on something as small as an exam—something that I have to do anyway—it's very encouraging if someone supports you and lets you know they believe you can do it.

—Cathy, 18, R.I.

Confidence is all you need to overcome any obstacle. It may sound trite, but believing in yourself is the key ingredient to accomplishing your goals. People can have all the smarts and skills in the world, but they'll never accomplish anything if they don't have the ability to use them. By letting people know you expect the best from them, you can help them deliver just that. Go beyond the generic. Be specific about why you have confidence in others:

Name names: Identify the specific traits that you think show a person's strength. Is your boyfriend stressed about his college interviews? Remind him that he charmed you with his sense of humor and his intelligence—especially about current events. Surely the college rep he meets will be equally impressed by his sophisticated worldview.

Give examples: Remind the person of past accomplishments: "I've seen you skateboard, so I know you're totally coordinated. Snowboarding uses more or less the same moves. You'll pick it up in no time."

Promise support: Let other people know you'll be right there with them, cheering them on until they accomplish their goal.

Which means you can give people an amazing gift: by letting them know you have faith in their abilities, you can strengthen their belief in themselves. Bringing out the best in others is what leadership is all about.

✳ WHEN ALL ELSE FAILS, THROW DOWN ✳

FEW PEOPLE CAN RESIST A GOOD CHALLENGE. Throw down a dare, and most of us can't resist picking it up. That can be a good thing or a bad thing. Used wisely, challenges can be a powerful tool for a leader. You can excite others' love of a challenge to their (and possibly your own) benefit, daring them to meet or exceed their highest expectations.

Are you the captain of your basketball team and looking for a way to get everyone more excited about practice? Why not suggest that whoever makes the most free throws during practice gets to chill while everyone else puts the equipment away, or gets to eat free at Friday's pizza party? You'll be amazed at how much a little competition gets people moving. The same strategy can help you motivate your boyfriend to get to work in the chemistry class you know he's barely passing. If you don't want to see him stuck in summer school, find a way to make learning worth his while. Dare him to earn a B. Tell him if he does he can pick the movies you two see for the next month, but if he doesn't he'll have to join you for at least four certified tearjerkers. Trust me, if the boy can do chemistry, he will show you now.

Is your gorgeous best friend too shy to talk to the guy she likes? Well, if letting her know that you think she's funny, smart, and beautiful—a catch by anyone's definition—isn't enough of a push, why not dare her to approach him herself? Let her in on the tips from chapter 4, and tell her to make eye contact, give him a big smile, and just say hi. She'll be a step closer to talking to him—and will probably get a big boost to her ego for doing something outside her comfort zone. Or you can make it a competition: if she smiles at the boy, you'll do something that's hard for you, like submitting the short

story she knows you have in your locker to the school paper, like you keep saying you will. As Dale Carnegie said, people love the game—the chance to prove their worth, to excel, and to win. So go ahead and throw down a challenge: dare people to be their best.

This holds true for you too. Remember back in chapter 1 when Atoosa Rubenstein, editor in chief of *Seventeen,* gave us a lesson in using others' negative energy as rocket fuel to do your best? The same holds true for those who want you to believe you can't accomplish something. Take it as a challenge. When Atoosa was given the chance to launch *Cosmo-GIRL* at just twenty-six, plenty of people were betting against her. She recalls, "After we'd been out for about a year and were successful, I did an interview with the *New York Post.* The reporter asked me how I felt considering nobody thought I could do it. I was just like, 'What do you mean? I had no idea.' But the truth is, when I hear stuff like that, it would make me even more determined to succeed. Suddenly there we were, my competitors were way down in sales and *Cosmo-GIRL* was way up." By looking at other people's doubts as a challenge instead of buying into them, Atoosa made *Cosmo-GIRL* one of the top-selling and most loved teen mags on newsstands today.

✳ BE A POSITIVE PEER ✳

AT THIS POINT IN YOUR LIFE you've probably heard all you ever want to hear about the pitfalls of peer pressure, so we'll skip the whole "If they jumped off a building, would you do it too?" speech. But it is worth looking at the positive side of peer pressure. The next time a friend comes to you to discuss a tough decision, flex your leadership skills and instead of just telling her your opinion, *show* her. Translation: if you want your friends to be loyal, be a loyal friend. If you want your boyfriend to be up-front with you, be open and honest with him. If you want your teammates to give their all, never miss a practice. If you want your little sister to stay away from drinking, drugs, and risky sex, start by making the right decisions yourself. When friends ask you for advice, instead of ranting about why they shouldn't do something, let them know how good it makes you feel to stick to your core beliefs. (Check out the exercise at the end of chapter 2 if you need a quick reference for those values.) Your message will sink in and may take root.

Sure, some friends may still choose to do things you wouldn't. But even so, you'll remind them of the confidence and self-respect that comes with making smart choices and being true to yourself. That's worth at least a million "I told you so's."

The other benefit: you'll bring out the best in yourself, too. If you're setting an example for your friends, siblings, and boyfriend, you'll step up to the plate, no matter what life throws at you. Instead of spending your life obsessing over superficial things like how you look or what activities are cool, you'll have a built-in motivation to do what's right for you. It's easy to go along with the crowd—and safe too. People don't pay much attention to you if you do what everyone else does. But that old saying "Nothing ventured, nothing gained"—well, it's true. You can spend your whole life playing it safe or you can take risks that distinguish you from the pack and make you a true role model. Ask yourself who you want to be. What values do you want to be a walking, breathing illustration of? Then expect no less of yourself.

✳ ACCEPT YOUR PERSONAL BEST ✳

IF YOU'VE TRIED YOUR BEST and really given your all, never berate yourself if you don't quite reach your loftiest ambitions. If you set the bar high enough, it may take you several tries to clear it—and that's okay. What's not okay is giving up at the first sign of failure or thinking of yourself as a loser. In chapter 7 you learned how mistakes can be opportunities for learning and help us grow as people. The same is true of failure. Doing your best is something to be proud of. It takes courage and character to be true to yourself and really push your limits.

When the U.S. women's national soccer team lost in overtime at the 2000 Olympics, they were understandably crushed. Led by Mia Hamm, one of the most talented players ever to grace the field, they'd expected to take home the gold just as they had at the 1996 games. By finishing second, some players felt they'd let themselves, their fans, and their country down. But Mia refused to let a success be turned into a defeat:

As we stood on the podium trying to face the world in defeat, a lot of my teammates could barely look up. The sadness of losing had clouded the reality: we had played a great tournament and a great game. We should be proud of our silver medals. I quietly stepped off the podium and walked around to each player and reminded her, "Hold your head high and be proud of what we've accomplished." As I got back on the podium, I looked down the row and saw my teammates facing the world with a collective smile. See, we didn't necessarily meet our expectation of winning a gold medal, but that day we realized that being the best doesn't always mean coming out on top. It means putting forth your best effort, something I have no doubt we did that day.

It's important to expect the best from yourself and others. But it's just as important to recognize and appreciate your achievements, even if they don't match your expectations. Remember, you don't need to "expect perfection," in which case you will always be disappointed. As a leader you need only to expect the best. It's all you can ask of anyone—including yourself. Give it your all and then take pride in knowing you did so. Others will see you for the winner that you are.

✳ IN THE KNOW ✳

BY NOW, you've learned a thing or two about human nature. Actually, you've learned eight things:

1. You don't gain anything by condemning, criticizing, or complaining—or by reacting negatively when you encounter the three Cs in others.

2. By praising the best in others, you can inspire them to live up to their full potential. And by living authentically and being true to your own values, you'll blossom into the person you most want to be.

3. The only way anyone will do anything is if you make them want to do it.

4. A smile and a genuine interest in someone new is all you need to make a friend.

5. The single most important way you can be a good friend, girlfriend, or daughter is to really listen to what the people in your life have to say.

6. You can't win an argument, but you can use common ground and questions to understand a situation better, shut down arguments, and open the road for discussion and compromise.

7. People aren't born cool or smart or sophisticated— you learn these traits through trial and error. If you make a mistake, admit it, do what you can to set things straight, and move on. You'll be a better person for it.

8. Be a leader. Expect the best from yourself and others, and you won't be disappointed.

These are the only skills you need to win friends and influence people. And they will be as important to your future success as any academic or extracurricular achievement— maybe more so. You can have the IQ of a rocket scientist or the moves of Britney Spears, but if you can't get along with people, you won't get very far, either professionally or personally. Even if at times you lack the right credentials, if you can win over others, you'll be unstoppable.

Dale Carnegie's principles have changed the lives of millions of people who have read his books and tried to live what they've learned. My hope is that this new edition, written especially for you, has given you insights that help you strengthen your relationships, reach your goals, and stand out as a leader in any group, now and for the rest of your life.

About Donna Dale Carnegie

DONNA DALE CARNEGIE is the daughter of Dale Carnegie, major shareholder and Chairman of the Board of Dale Carnegie & Associates. As heir to her father's books, she feels a special commitment to sharing his work with a wider audience, which he would have done if he were living today.

She lives in Portland, Oregon, and is also a professional artist specializing in landscape paintings and horses, her life-long passion.

About Dale Carnegie Training®

FOUNDED IN 1912, Dale Carnegie Training has evolved from one man's belief in the power of self-improvement to a performance-based training company with offices worldwide. It focuses on giving people in business the opportunity to sharpen their skills and improve their performance to build positive, steady, and profitable results. *(Additionally, we have expanded our offerings to meet the needs of young individuals who can benefit from our programs as they shape themselves for future success—see the teen section on page 189.)*

Headquartered on Long Island, New York, Dale Carnegie Training is represented in all fifty of the United States and in more than sixty-five countries. Dale Carnegie Training has dedicated itself to serving the business community worldwide.

Dale Carnegie Training developed the concept of business training. From leadership training to relationship selling, from presentation skills to teamwork development, Dale Carnegie Training designs and delivers programs that provide a practical approach for business success in a competitive environment.

We believe that every business is a collection of individuals who have come together to pursue a common objective. Therefore, the success of any business depends on the success of the individuals in it.

Dale Carnegie Training emphasizes practical principles and processes by designing programs that offer people the knowledge, skills, and practices they need to add value to their business. Connecting proven solutions with real-world challenges, Dale Carnegie Training is recognized internationally as the leader in bringing out the best in people.

Dale Carnegie's original body of knowledge has been constantly updated, expanded, and refined through nearly a century's worth of real-life business experiences. The 160 Carnegie Managing Directors around the world use their training and consulting services with companies of all sizes in all business segments to increase knowledge and performance. The result of this collective, global experience is an expanding reservoir of business acumen that our clients rely on to drive business results.

Working directly with companies and individuals, Dale Carnegie Training offers programs tailored to specific client needs and strategies. The focus is on the challenges people and organizations face every day as they implement current business goals and long-range vision.

What differentiates Dale Carnegie Training is its unique four-phase training cycle that integrates these components: *attitude change, knowledge, practice,* and *skill development.* Newly learned principles evolve into acquired lifelong skills that produce long-term behavioral change.

Leading corporations in diverse industries—telecommunications, banking, retail, manufacturing, consulting, medical services—have testified to the performance gains that Dale Carnegie Training has generated within their organizations. Companies can choose from comprehensive course material or receive customized training targeted at very specific business goals. They report that Dale Carnegie Training offers organizations a competitive edge in the global marketplace by developing the skills needed to build both internal and external relationships—transforming customers into business partners.

Dale Carnegie Training® for Teens

TODAY the world is more complex, competitive, and demanding than ever before. Young people often need to balance school, work, and relationships, while at the same time working and planning for their future.

Our program is designed to prepare young people for the real world. It gives them the skills they need to reach their goals and live up to their full potential—at school, home, and work.

At Dale Carnegie Training, we call them "skills that will last a lifetime." The program content focuses on five key areas that are critical for future success:

- building self-confidence

- enhancing communication skills

- interpersonal skill development

- teamwork and leadership skills

- effective attitude management

Visit Dale Carnegie Training at www.dalecarnegie.com to find the office nearest you.